CRAFTING THE
PERSONAL
ESSAY

WRITER'S DIGEST
BOOKS

writing the personal essay is like chasing mental rabbits

CRAFTING THE
PERSONAL
ESSAY

A GUIDE FOR
WRITING AND PUBLISHING
CREATIVE NONFICTION

DINTY W. MOORE

Writer's Digest Books
An imprint of Penguin Random House LLC
penguinrandomhouse.com

Printed in the United States of America

ISBN 978-1-58297-796-6

Edited by Scott Francis
Designed by Terri Woesner
Cover illustration © stockimages.com

dedication

For Susan A. Moore Smith
with love and gratitude

about the author

Photo by Renita M. Romasco

Dinty W. Moore is the author of the 2008 memoir *Between Panic & Desire* (University of Nebraska), termed a "quirky, entertaining joyride" by *Publishers Weekly*. His other books include *The Accidental Buddhist*, *Toothpick Men*, and *The Emperor's Virtual Clothes*.

Moore's books have been translated and released in German, Italian, and Chinese editions, and he has published essays and stories in *The Southern Review*, *The Georgia Review*, *Harpers*, *The New York Times Sunday Magazine*, *The Philadelphia Inquirer Magazine*, *Gettysburg Review*, *Utne Reader*, and *Crazyhorse*, among numerous other venues.

A professor of nonfiction writing at Ohio University, Moore has won many awards for his writing, including a National Endowment for the Arts Fellowship in Fiction.

Moore was born in Erie, Pennsylvania, and holds degrees from the University of Pittsburgh and Louisiana State University.

He can be reached at panic.desire@gmail.com.

TABLE OF CONTENTS

PART ONE
WRITING THE ESSAY

PART TWO
REACHING READERS

INTRODUCTION:
THE PERSONAL ESSAY, HERE AND NOW

"Fill your paper with the breathings of your heart."
—William Wordsworth

The personal essay is perhaps the oldest form of nonfiction prose, and yet it remains one of the most commonly misunderstood. Some people persist in the belief that the essay needs to be antiquated and moldy, while others claim the essay must follow a menu of one hundred creativity-destroying rules.

These misperceptions are unfortunate, because the personal essay is a wonderfully flexible and creative form, as fresh and inventive as the writer wishes it to be. In addition, the essay remains an ideal vehicle for satisfying that human urge so many of us feel—to not just live year to year but to capture a bit of that life, to produce an enduring record of our better thoughts.

That is, after all, why so many people—young and old, homemaker and trial lawyer, working and retired—share the dream of being writers, of having others delight and marvel at what has been written.

We want to speak. And we want to be heard.

USING THIS BOOK

Crafting the Personal Essay: A Guide for Writing and Publishing Creative Nonfiction is designed to clear up the confusion about the form and encourage writers at all levels of experience to explore the flexibility and power of the personal essay, as it exists here and now. This book is meant to be a hands-on, creativity-expanding guide, intended to encourage new energy and fresh paths in your writing.

Part One includes key chapters isolating important elements of the essayist's way of seeing and thinking alongside briefer chapters which isolate specific modes of essay writing, such as the lyric, the spiritual, and the gastronomic essay.

Part Two focuses on reaching potential readers, with chapters on establishing a regular writing routine, on revision, and on strategies for publication.

My suggestion is that you work through these pages slowly, with pencil in hand. I have provided more than one hundred prompts and writing exercises, and though it is unlikely that each and every one of them will spark you into action, my hope is that many of them will. Take the time to scribble your responses to the prompts, or to the examples provided in the various chapters, and save the notes and paragraphs you create. When you are done reading and writing your way through these chapters, you may find that you have a stack of essays waiting to be completed.

I will be suggesting various dos and don'ts along the way, and regularly alerting you to possible pitfalls, but there are really only two firm imperatives:

- You must always keep an open mind, be willing to explore, and

- Always be careful to bring your reader along on your journey. Writing is indeed a solo act, but the result is meant to be shared.

So let's get started.

writing the personal
essay
is like chasing
mental
rabbits

PART ONE
WRITING THE
ESSAY

THE GENTLE ART OF THE PERSONAL ESSAY

One reason the essay is so misunderstood nowadays may be that well-intentioned but overburdened writing teachers from grade school through college have tried to drill us in the essay "form," but in the end this instruction often amounted to little more than a series of awkward limitations.

Remember, for instance, the five-paragraph essay? In this boxcar-boxcar-caboose approach, the essay often seemed to have more thesis sentences than it did interesting ideas. Not only was the essay supposed to follow a strict outline, but every essay was supposed to follow the same strict outline, forever and ever, amen.

No wonder we were turned off.

Or how about the college admissions essay, that uncomfortable exercise in clumsy self-aggrandizement? "As a freshman, I helped decorate the gymnasium for our Spring Dance. In my sophomore year, I saved the world ..."

And then, of course, there was the dreaded research essay, a form that is expected—no, actually required—to be as dry and tasteless as day-old toast. I'm starting to choke just thinking about it.

Well, here's the good news: The personal essay is none of these.

⏱ WRITING EXERCISE: GET IT OUT OF YOUR SYSTEM!

Take a few minutes to scribble down any recollections of what you've learned over the years about the essay form. This is a good time to vent: about teachers who throttled your creativity, supervisors at work who thought good writing had to be deadly dull and impenetrable, or any sorts of misguided notions that made you turn away from what you really wanted to write.

Or if you were lucky enough to encounter one of those wonderful teachers who added fuel to your writing passion, take a moment to celebrate that fine soul.

What did you want to write then? What do you want to write now?

THE GENTLE ART

So the essay is not a tedious freight train full of dreary thesis sentences, mind-numbing citations, and predictably stale conclusions. Then what is it?

The answer is simple enough.

The personal essay is, of course, *personal*, meaning of you, from your unique point-of-view. And it is an "*assay*," derived from a French word meaning "to try" or "to attempt."

Here the essence of the form is found: The personal essayist (that would be you) takes a topic—virtually any topic under the big yellow sun—and holds it up to the bright light, turning it this way and that, upside and down, studying every perspective, fault, and reflection, in an artful attempt to perceive something fresh and significant. But it is always an effort, a trial, not a lecture or diatribe. The essayist *does not sit down at her desk already knowing all*

■■■

of the right answers, because if she did, there would be no reason to write.

In other words, the personal essay is a gentle art, an idiosyncratic combination of the author's discrete sensibilities and the endless possibilities of meaning and connection. The essay is graceful, wise, and always surprising. The essay invites extreme playfulness and almost endless flexibility.

Or as Annie Dillard has written of the essay form:

"There's nothing you cannot do with it; no subject matter is forbidden, no structure is proscribed. You get to make up your own structure every time, a structure that arises from the materials and best contains them. The material is the world itself, which, so far, keeps on keeping on."

 WRITING EXERCISE: WHY DO YOU WRITE?

Listen just a moment to Terry Tempest Williams, from her essay "Why I Write":

> I write to discover. I write to uncover. I write to
> meet my ghosts ... I write because it is dangerous,
> a bloody risk, like love, to form the words ...
> I write as though I am whispering in the ear
> of the one I love.

Now ask yourself the same question. You can answer more directly, or mimic Tempest Williams' lyric voice, or perhaps pretend that you are whispering into the ear of someone you love. But take five minutes and just explore the question.

Why do *you* write?

Crafting the Personal Essay

THE PERSONAL
(NOT PRIVATE) ESSAY

"I sit here in silence writing this small volume of words, and it seems to me the most public thing I ever have done."
—Richard Rodriguez

If you've been part of a writing group, you've no doubt encountered the writer who shares his work with others in the room, sits back for what he assumes will be unceasing praise, and then grows indignant when someone suggests that his words are not clear enough to make what he intends fully obvious.

"Well, *I* understood it," he might snort. "It makes total sense to *me*."

Perhaps this writer is just reacting out of insecurity (yes, insecurity is a trait most, if not all, of us share), but let's examine for a moment the logic behind his defensive retort.

Each of us has a miraculous mind full of associations, ideas, and richly remembered experiences. If we are writing out of our childhood, that childhood may be as vivid in our memory as a movie we have watched fifteen, twenty, or one hundred times. The old brown sofa, layered with blankets, which sat against the far wall of our grandparents' living room, is available as a full and clear mental picture in an instant. So is the soothing lilt of our grandmother's voice. The onion and olive oil smell of her kitchen.

We can see it. We were there.

But all that our readers have—without our carefully crafted assistance—is what you are looking at right now:

A WHITE PAGE
COVERED WITH
BLACK SYMBOLS

In our highly visual culture—television, movies, videos on an iPad—it is important to remember just how magical good writing can be. It is an act of alchemy, really, this ability of our best writers to transform the abstract lines and circles that represent the twenty-six letters of the alphabet into vivid, too-real-to-be-forgotten experiences.

And even if we aren't writing from memory—if instead we are trying to string together an extended metaphor or to explain a particularly complex sequence of assumptions leading to a logical conclusion—remember that we as authors arrive at an understanding of our words and intentions well before the reader. It is our job to transfer what we've seen, remembered, reasoned, or imagined. If the reader does not comprehend, we have failed to do our task well.

The best writing also provokes an emotional reaction, be it laughter, sadness, joy, or indignation. Keep in mind, though, that there exists a vast difference between those thoughts, ideas, and memories that elicit a powerful reaction from you, the writer, and those that will have the desired impact on someone who does not know you or have a stake in your well-being. Certain "private" sentences may seem exhilarating to write and to reread as you edit your early drafts, but if they don't transmit that same emotional or intellectual experience to an anonymous reader, then they are not doing the job.

Author Kathleen Norris suggests that what we are looking for, in the exchange between writer and reader, is resonance.

To be resonant, Norris informs us, "is to be 'strong and deep in tone, resounding.' And to resound means to be filled to the depth with a sound that is sent back to its source. An essay that works is similar; it gives back to the reader a thought, a memory, an emotion made richer by the experience of another. Such an essay may confirm the reader's sense of things, or it may contradict it. But always, and in glorious, mysterious ways that the author cannot control, it begins to belong to the reader."

This basic lesson—remembering the reader who will see your words—is something you probably know already, but it is also something worth reminding ourselves of on a daily basis. We might do well to write "Remember the Reader" on an index card and tape it to our computer monitors.

So remember, though personal, the essay is never meant to be private.

Privacy is for your diary.

Essays are for readers.

WRITING EXERCISE: THE FLOOD OF MEMORY

Acclaimed novelist Toni Morrison likens memory to the way the Mississippi River, years after being straightened and pushed into levees by the Army Corps of Engineers, still strains at times to flood its banks and revisit the original, meandering route. "All water has a perfect memory and is forever trying to get back to where it was," Morrison tells us. "Writers are like that: remembering where we were, what valley we ran through, what the banks were like, the light that was there and the route back to our original place."

I have worked with so many writers who worry that memory is not sharp enough, exact enough, or reliable enough for them to capture childhood moments with any authority, and, of course, science has proven the fallibility of memory time and time again. But what can we do, as writers?

It has been my experience that most of us remember more than we think that we do. It just takes some time to stop, think, and take our minds back to the original riverbanks. Once we have latched on to one memory—the color of the tablecloth on Aunt Jean's holiday table and the old-fashioned centerpiece she inherited from her grandmother, perhaps—that tiny foothold of memory is often the impetus to remember something else—the gravy boat that always spilled. Those two seemingly insignificant memories can help to unloosen yet another, and then another, small detail. These past moments are in your mind still, Morrison is telling us, just as the past lives in the memory of a river. Bringing it to the front just takes time.

Crafting the Personal Essay

In the end, all we promise the reader is that we have done our absolute best to fact-check our memories, and that we have tried our darndest to be accurate. Smart readers know that no other guarantee is necessary or possible.

So, go to the river of memory. Find one small detail, and start writing for just ten minutes, trying to remember one small detail at a time. See where it takes you today.

WRITING THE READER-FRIENDLY ESSAY

Good writing is never merely about following a set of directions. Like all artists of any form, essay writers occasionally find themselves breaking away from tradition or common practice in search of a fresh approach. Rules, as they say, are meant to be broken.

But even groundbreakers learn by observing what has worked before. If you are not already in the habit of reading other writers with an analytical eye, start forming that habit now. When you run across a moment in someone else's writing that seems somehow electric on the page, stop, go back, reread the section more slowly, and ask yourself, "What did she do here, put into this, or leave out, that makes it so successful?"

Similarly and often just as important, if you are reading a piece of writing and find yourself confused, bored, or frustrated, stop again, back up, squint closely at the writing, and form a theory as to how, when, or where the prose went bad.

Identifying the specific successful moves made by others increases the number of arrows in your quiver, ready for use when you sit down to start your own writing. Likewise, identifying the missteps in other writers' work makes you better at identifying the missteps in your own.

So, with that in mind, on to the suggestions.

Remember the Streetcar

Tennessee Williams' wonderful play, *A Streetcar Named Desire*, comes from a real streetcar in New Orleans and an actual neighborhood named Desire. In Williams' day, you could see the streetcar downtown with a lighted sign at the front telling folks where the vehicle was headed. The playwright saw this streetcar regularly—and also saw, of course, the metaphorical possibilities of the name.

Though this streetcar no longer runs, there is still a bus called Desire in New Orleans, and you've certainly seen streetcars or buses in other cities with similar, if less evocative, destination indicators: Uptown, Downtown, Shadyside, West End, Prospect Park.

People need to know what streetcar they are getting onto, you see, because they want to know where they will be when the streetcar stops and lets them off.

Excuse the rather basic transportation lesson, but it explains my first suggestion. An essay needs a lighted sign right up front telling the reader where they are going. Otherwise, the reader will be distracted and nervous at each stop along the way, unsure of the destination, not at all able to enjoy the ride.

Now there are dull ways of putting up your lighted sign:

This essay is about the death of my beloved dog.

Or:

Let me tell you about what happened to me last week.

And there are more artful ways.

Readers tend to appreciate the more artful ways.

For instance, let us look at how Richard Rodriguez opens his startling essay "Mr. Secrets":

> Shortly after I published my first autobiographical essay seven years ago, my mother wrote me a letter pleading with me never again to write about our family life. "Write about something else in the future. Our family life is private." And besides: "Why do you need to tell the *gringos* about how 'divided' you feel from the family?" I sit at my desk now, surrounded by versions of paragraphs and pages of this book, considering that question.

Where is the lighted streetcar sign in that paragraph?

Well, consider that Rodriguez has

- introduced the key characters who will inhabit his essay: himself and his mother,

- informed us that writing is central to his life,

- clued us in that this is also a story of immigration and assimilation (*gringos*), and

- provided us with the central question he will be considering throughout the piece: Why does he feel compelled to tell strangers the ins and outs of his conflicted feelings?

These four elements—generational conflict between author and parent, the isolation of a writer, cultural norms and difference, and the question of what is public and what is private—pretty much describe the heart of Rodriguez's essay.

Or to put it another way, at every stop along the way—each paragraph, each transition—we are on a streetcar passing through these four thematic neighborhoods, and Rodriguez has given us a map so we can follow along.

Stay on Track (More or Less)

The lighted streetcar sign is just the start. The reader needs travel assistance all along the journey. I'm going to switch metaphors here, however, because a streetcar is confined to a set of rigid parallel tracks, whereas the essay has more room to roam.

So let's look at this again: Imagine yourself in a foreign city, Budapest or San Miguel de Allende, with a tour guide leading you up and down cobblestone streets, through narrow alleys, around blind corners. If you feel confident that the tour guide knows his territory and has a clear itinerary—even if it is unspoken—then you will relax and fully enjoy the tour. If instead you start to distrust the tour guide (*"Is he lost? Did he forget where he is taking me? Can I trust him?"*), then you will become unsettled, distracted, and start paying less attention to the landscape and more to your concerns.

In that metaphor, you, the writer, are the tour guide, and the potentially nervous tourist is your reader. The landscape is the writing you have spent so much time crafting and perfecting.

I'll talk more about the meandering nature of the essay, and the freedom to roam from point to point, in the upcoming chapters, but for now I'll just remind you that there are ways to roam without seeming lost. So give your reader no reason to be tense. Let her feel constantly as if she is in competent hands.

Then, and only then, is her undivided attention on your words and images.

Find a Healthy Distance

Another important step in making your personal essay public not private is finding a measure of distance from your experience, learning to stand back, narrow your eyes, and scrutinize your own life with a dose of hale and hearty skepticism.

Why is finding a distance important? Because the private essay hides the author. The personal essay reveals. And to reveal means to let us see what is truly there, warts and all.

The truth about human nature is that we are all imperfect, sometimes messy, usually uneven individuals, and the moment you try to present yourself as a cardboard character—always right, always upstanding (or always wrong, a total mess)—the reader begins to doubt everything you say. Even if the reader cannot articulate his discomfort, he knows on a gut level that your perfect (or perfectly awful) portrait of yourself has to be false.

And then you've lost the reader.

Rodriguez's "Mr. Secrets" goes on from the opening paragraph to a wide-raging examination of his life. He shares with us the embarrassment he felt at times over the poverty of his family. He illuminates for us the difference it made when he went away to school and embraced a life of books and education. At the same time, he acknowledges how this education, and the public life he has chosen, often distances him from those he loves.

Eventually he circles directly back to his mother's opening question, and his central idea:

> It is to those whom my mother refers to as the
> *gringos* that I write. The *gringos*. The expression
> reminds me that she and my father have not fol-
> lowed their children all the way down the path to
> full Americanization.

It is worth noting what straightforward language Rodriguez employs throughout his piece. He is a highly educated
man with a considerable, and in fact, bilingual, vocabulary,
but he reveals these highly personal details with only the
simplest of sentences and words. Novice writers often trip
themselves up trying to sound weighty or cerebral, but the
truth is that expressing yourself in simpler words requires
more craftsmanship and skill than using multisyllabic, flow-
ery language, and it almost always works better.

Eventually Rodriguez works his essay to a key scene, a
moment when he is no longer just mulling over the conflicted
feelings brought on by his mother's written wishes but is visiting her in her home. While standing at her ironing board,
she asks him an odd question, "What is psychiatry?"

And Rodriguez writes:

> As a result of nothing we have been saying, her
> question has come. But I am not surprised by it.
> My mother and father ask me such things. Now
> that they are retired they seem to think about
> subjects they never considered before.

Rodriguez then shares with the reader his frustrated attempt to explain Freud and analysis to his mother, and how
he, upon realizing that his mother cannot comprehend his
words, finally uses the comparison of a Catholic priest hearing confession, something he knows his mother will understand because of her deep faith.

This makes sense finally, so his mother then asks, "You mean that people tell a psychiatrist about their personal lives?"

After which, Rodriguez writes:

> Even as I begin to respond, I realize that she can-
> not imagine ever doing such a thing. She shakes
> her head sadly, bending over the ironing board to
> inspect a shirt with the tip of the iron she holds
> in her hand.

This is an excellent example of what it means for a writer to stand back, narrow his eyes, and scrutinize his own life, with no agenda other than finding some truth. Rodriguez is illustrating the uncomfortable distance between himself and the woman he loves so deeply, his mother. He is not claiming her to be a saint, or himself as the best son any mother ever had, nor is he painting a gruesome picture of angry child or lousy parent. He is simply calling it the way it is, or the way, at least, that he sees it when he takes the time to reflect in detail, and when he is honest with himself.

He is Americanized. His mother to a large extent is not. She has had little schooling. He has had a good amount. She embraces the Catholicism of her ancestors. He does not in the same way. Inevitably, these people, despite their love, are going to feel some disconnection.

Those of us in Rodriguez's shoes—and that would be so many readers, whether our parents were first-generation, second-, or third-, Mexican, Italian, Irish, or Greek—are going to recognize this.

Rodriguez recognizes it, poignantly, and with clarity, in the final image, when his mother "shakes her head sadly," and bends "over the ironing board to inspect a shirt with the tip of the iron she holds in her hand."

It is all there.

WRITING EXERCISE: GESTURE

Though we do not know and cannot know what is going through the mind of Richard Rodriguez's aging mother in the scenes he gives us, we can certainly make our own assumptions based on embedded clues, such as the moment where she shakes her head sadly and bends over the ironing board. Those two actions speak volumes within the context of Rodriguez's essay.

In truth, it is often the small gestures that convey the most meaning. When we are angry, bombastically waving our arms, kicking the car door, our gestures are meaningless, really, because anyone can tell that we are angry simply by listening to our raised voices and registering our heated words.

But when we have private feelings and thoughts, or when we think that we are hiding our reactions, little gestures often reveal our true selves.

Try to capture some of these small gestures on the page. How did *your* mother register disappointment? If she was angry at someone in your family—your father perhaps—but wanted to hide that anger, how did it come out anyway? If you have a sister or brother, how (when you were younger) did you know that they were telling a fib? How can you tell now?

Or think about your son or daughter, if you have them. Part of being a parent is to closely watch our children for signs, signals, small indications of what might be going on inside their mysterious brains.

Gesture is only a small tool in your descriptive toolbox, but it can be one of the most powerful. Practice seeing them, and capturing them on the page, and pretty soon you won't have to explain anything to your reader. They will see it all for themselves.

Pursue the Deeper Truth

The best writers never settle for the insight they find on the surface of whatever subject they are exploring. They are constantly trying to lift the surface layer, to see what interesting ideas or questions might lie beneath.

To illustrate, let's look at another exemplary essay, "Silence the Pianos," by Floyd Skloot.

Here is his opening:

> A year ago today, my mother stopped eating. She was ninety-six, and so deep in her dementia that she no longer knew where she was, who I was, who she herself was. All but the last few seconds had vanished from the vast scroll of her past.

Essays exploring a loved one's decline into dementia or the painful loneliness of a parent's death are among the most commonly seen by editors of magazines and judges of essay contests. There is a good reason for this: These events can truly shake us to our core. But too often, when writing about such a significant loss, the writer focuses on the idea that what has happened is not fair and that the loved one who is no longer around is so deeply missed.

Are these emotions true?

Yes, they are.

Are they interesting for a reader?

Often, they simply are not.

The problem is that there are certain things readers already know, and that would include the idea that the loss of a loved one to death or dementia is a deep wound, that it seems not fair when such heartbreak occurs, and that we oftentimes find ourselves regretting not having spent more time with the lost loved one.

These reactions seem truly significant when they occur in our own lives, and revisiting them in our writing allows us to experience those powerful feelings once again. For this reason it is hard to grasp that the account of our loss might have little or no impact on a reader who did not know this loved one, or does not know you, and who does not have the emotional reaction already in the gut.

In other words, there are certain "private" moments that feel exhilarating to revisit, and "private" sentences that seem stirring to write and to reread as we edit our early drafts, but they are not going to have the same effect in the public arena of publishable prose.

Skloot knows this, and his instinct is to pursue those aspects of his story that are more difficult to reveal, further below his surface feelings, and thus more surprising to the reader.

He goes on after the opening sentences to describe, with both love and pain, the final moment he spent with his mother before her death. He and his wife Beverly sang to her by the bedside, old songs that she loved, even though there was no visible evidence that his mother was aware or could hear the words. But then, for just a moment, she opened her eyes, looked at her adult son, and then shut them again. "I felt sure," the author writes, "that nothing had registered in her mind, but was glad for the last glimpse we shared as the song ended. I knew then it was time for silence."

His essay widens out further here.

He takes us to the cemetery, recounts his daughter's loving eulogy, which leads him to remember W. H. Auden's poem "Funeral Blues":

> Stop all the clocks, cut off the telephone,
> Prevent the dog from barking with a juicy bone,
> Silence the pianos and with muffled drum
> Bring out the coffin, let the mourners come.

It is the middle line, "silence the pianos," that Skloot tells us brought him to tears days later, as the weight of his mother's life and death finally settled in.

> ... I found myself imagining my mother in her heyday, seated at the piano and banging out one of her signature songs, Gershwin or Rodgers and Hart. Her stout body would rise off the bench, her eyes would close, and she would lean way over to the right, straining to reach the notes for her grand finale.

Her piano is silenced, he realizes, and though someone with less doubt might imagine his mother now banging the ivory keys in heaven, the truth is that the author has always been unsure of his belief in an afterlife. As comforting as images of heaven and harp-playing angels can be to the grieving, Skloot tells his readers, he has never fully trusted in them, and in fact he is not sure what to make of the afterlife.

His essay explores these doubts and uncertainties, as a man mourning his mother's passing, and also as a man who will someday die himself, as we all do. He digs deeper and deeper into the experience, looking for something fresh he can bring to the reader.

I will not summarize Skloot's entire essay here, since truly beautiful writing can never be done justice by a summary, but instead let me share with you the last few words, where the writer revisits the family cemetery plot seven months later. Notice that he does not resolve his doubts or reach some conclusion to his grief. Instead, he tries only to put us inside of his experience, to show to us and help us to feel how he carries his heartache forward, and moves on.

> As we began to leave the gravesite, I turned back as though summoned, and took a long, hard look. Clock time seemed to stop, but I felt myself in the presence of another kind of time altogether, remembering trips to this place with my father and brother when I was a boy and only my grandparents' graves were there. In the distance, a church bell rang, and its fading sound was like one of my mother's great concluding piano chords. Beverly laced her arm through mine and drew me close, standing with me in the silence that followed.

 ## WRITING EXERCISE: THE FULL WEIGHT

If you have lost someone close to you, a parent maybe, you know that the full weight of the loss doesn't come at the funeral home or at the cemetery—the full weight arrives two or three days later, when you look around and that beloved person is not there. Maybe it hits when you pick up the phone out of sheer habit to share some family news with your mother and realize she won't be answering. Or when you go into the office and your best friend's desk is empty. For some of us, the lost loved one might be a loyal pet, and the truth is the same. It takes a while to sink in.

If you have such a moment to share, try to capture it now on the page. Don't dwell on the funeral or your tears or those moments when you were too shocked or numb to even register your own feelings. Instead, write about that disorienting moment later in the week when you weren't surrounded by loved ones and neighbors with consoling words, when you weren't distracted by funeral arrangements, when no one was watching, and it hit you, the full realization that this person (or pet) you loved so much would not be walking in the door.

Don't worry for the moment what essay you are writing or what your larger meaning may be. Just try to capture it.

MY ASSAY: WHEREIN THE AUTHOR ATTEMPTS TO FOLLOW HIS OWN ADVICE

At the same time that I am composing the personal essay writing guide that you have in your hands right now, I am also trying to *assay* a short look at the importance of walking, an essay I've tentatively titled "On Foot." At times, to be honest, I have both documents open on my desktop and will occasionally jump back and forth. One project inevitably informs the other.

So, for instance, if it is my goal to send a clear signal to the reader as to where I am headed (like that streetcar sign), perhaps my essay should begin here:

> I arrived in Boca Raton, Florida, as naïve as Christopher Columbus when he first stumbled off the

Santa Maria thinking he had landed on East Indian
shores. I had visions of walking along serene Boca
beaches, of leaping dolphins and brilliant shells,
of encountering the occasional native under a
palm tree and exchanging pleasantries about life
in the slow-paced beachfront paradise.

Of course, I knew nothing.

And as for paradise, I hope never to return.

Like Rodriguez, I am introducing the two main characters
(myself and the city of Boca Raton). I am also establishing a
somewhat lighthearted naiveté for my own persona (more
about persona in chapter twelve) and hinting, perhaps, at
the underlying tension in the essay, my preconceived notions of a place versus the reality that I find.

Throughout the rest of this writing guide, I will attempt
to directly apply my own advice to the essay-in-progress and
will share with you how this advice works (or does not) in
pushing the work toward becoming more reader friendly.

And by the way, if you'd like to read the final version of
my walking essay, it can be found at the end of this book, in
the Appendix.

FINAL THOUGHTS ABOUT
THE READER-FRIENDLY ESSAY

In the last twenty years of teaching writing, the most valuable lesson that I have found myself able to share is the need
for us as writers to step outside of our own thoughts, to
imagine an audience made up of real people on the other
side of the page. This audience does not know us, they are
not by default eager to read what we have written, and
though thoughtful literate readers are by and large good

people with large hearts, they have no intrinsic stake in whatever problems (or joys) we have in our lives.

This is the public, the readers you want to invite into your work.

Self-expression may be the beginning of writing, but it should never be the endpoint. Only by focusing on these anonymous readers, by acknowledging that you are creating something for them, something that has value, something that will enrich their existence and make them glad to have read what you have written, will you find a way to truly reach your audience.

And *that*—truly reaching your audience and offering them something of value—is perhaps as good a definition of successful writing as I've ever heard.

WRITING THE MEMOIR ESSAY

"One writes out of only one thing—one's own experience. Everything depends on how relentlessly one forces from this experience the last drop, sweet or bitter, it can possibly give."
—James Baldwin

A student in one of my classes some years back had been taught the prevailing notion that a writer should never use *I* in their writing. It has never been clear to me why so many teachers insist on passing this rule along, although perhaps it has to do with the idea that avoiding that perpendicular pronoun leads to a more authoritative voice. In other words, the sentence "I think that everyone should recycle ..." is seen as less weighty than the sentence "Recycling is necessary for the planet and one should therefore support the local community's efforts to begin such a praiseworthy program."

Fair enough, if you are writing a letter to the editor, but unfortunately for my student, the assignment for that day was to write out of personal experience, and more specifically to describe "a private location, in your home perhaps, where you feel the safest and most secure."

The poor girl, earnest but confounded, came in that morning and began to read her opening paragraph aloud to the entire class:

"When one enters my bedroom and snuggles into the thick pile of spreads and comforters on my four-poster bed, one can't help but feel pure contentment. When one reaches down to feel the cottony softness of my newly washed pajamas ..."

Well, it only took a few moments for the bad-mannered boys in class to start snickering. Boys being boys, they were drawn to the idea of slipping into the young woman's four-poster bed and feeling the cottony softness of her pajamas, but of course that's not at all what she intended.

I did my best to soothe her embarrassment and used the awkward moment to remind students that the idea of never using *I* in writing is simply bad advice, often leading to clumsy, circuitous constructions.

The memoir essay is all about the *I*, not just as a source of insight, but as the subject itself. There is no shame in using yourself as subject, and no need to hide that fact behind some veil of objectivity and erudition.

The *I* stands tall and proud.

So, what is this memoir essay?

Memoir, obviously, has to do with memory, and though that might mean writing about an event in your childhood, it is well worth remembering that you are by no means so limited. A successful memoir essay might be written about the two years you spent just out of high school working in a small town five-and-dime (back when every small town had a five-and-dime), or it could relate the story of your successful two-year battle with cancer at age forty. You could write a memoir at age seventy looking only at the previous five years and the adventure of building your perfect retirement beach house on Costa Rica's Nicoya Peninsula. Memoir simply means it happened in the past.

Often, when nonfiction is taught or studied, memoir and the personal essay are placed apart, as separate genres, but the truth is that these two strands have considerable overlap. In theory, one might write memoir and not essay; if, for instance, all that you did was re-create previous events from memory, with absolutely no embellishment or reflection. In practice, however, writers almost never do this. They re-create the past and then reflect on what they have learned, or haven't learned, about what now makes sense or what continues to be a mystery.

This use of personal experience for reflection—not just "this happened to me," but "this happened and it gave me occasion to ponder"—distinguishes that thin line between pure memoir and the memoir essay.

Or as James Baldwin reminds us, we are always writing from our own experience, but it is up to us and indeed, our responsibility as writers—to squeeze from our experience "the last drop, sweet or bitter, it can possibly give."

A Note on Navel-Gazing

Nonfiction writing of all sorts has flourished recently—evidence can be found in book sales and in magazines ranging all the way from your local college's literary journal to the pages of Oprah's *O*. True stories well told are everywhere—and much appreciated.

Strangely, though, during this same span of years, memoir and creative nonfiction have been under almost unyielding attack.

One of the highest-profile assaults came in 1997, when James Wolcott, writing in *Vanity Fair,* asserted that memoir craze was nothing more than "... a big, earnest blob of me-first sensibility ... a pierced-navel-gazing orgy ... [and] a journalism of the self ... reaching for a phantom nipple."

Those are some colorful (and *cheap*) shots taken by Wolcott, and perhaps they should be ignored, but at about the same time, *New York Times* book reviewer Michiko Kakutani wrote that "The current memoir craze has fostered the belief that confession is therapeutic, that therapy is redemptive and that redemption equals art, and it has encouraged the delusion that candor, daring and shamelessness are substitutes for craft, that the exposed life is the same thing as an examined one."

Wolcott and Kakutani are clearly of the opinion that contemporary nonfiction writers are too concerned with their own well-being and that this concern for the self is somehow poison on the page. They have used this claim as a bludgeon to denigrate the entire genre of creative nonfiction, and every six months or so, some new critic commences a fresh attack, often using the words of Wolcott or Kakutani as a launching pad.

As in almost all complex matters, the critics are right and wrong.

They are right that it is not enough to simply expose your life, or describe your pain or triumph, as if what you were after was mere attention and acknowledgment. But they are wrong to suggest that most of what is published as memoir suffers from this deficiency.

Memoir is not about "look at me, look at me," at least not when done well. Instead it is about trying to understand the vexing mysteries of human existence. Yes, that might sound a bit highfalutin and ambitious, but it's true.

Though science, psychology, and religion offer various explanations and ways to comprehend why we exist as human beings, how we might have arrived, and how best to behave ourselves during the time allotted, the simple fact is that most of us walk around day-to-day filled with questions. Why do bad things happen to good people? And why, for that matter, do good things happen to clearly bad people? And if sages and prophets have been telling us for thousands of years that the simple recipe for happiness is love and contentment, why are so many of us lonely and unfulfilled?

These questions may have no immediate answers, but reading about other people's lives, other people's challenges, and other people's small victories gives the reader fresh perspectives, i.e., more ways to consider the questions at hand.

Listen for a moment to Sue William Silverman, author of the memoir *Love Sick: One Woman's Journey through Sexual Addiction*, a book that was recently featured as a Lifetime movie:

> What most distresses me is when memoirs, especially those written by women, are labeled 'confessional.' In effect, these critics are implying that women's memoirs are nothing more than navel gazing, that they have no literary merit ... When I write about recovering from incest or sexual addiction, I'm also writing about loss, alienation, identity. Aren't these universal themes to which most anyone can relate? Aren't these also social issues, part of what society struggles with on a daily basis—so not navel gazing at all.

Three Quick Tips

- When writing your memoir essay, remember the crucial importance of details. Don't tell us what happened, show us. Don't just claim that Uncle Clem was a kooky prankster; show him blowing up your family's garbage cans on the Fourth of July. Don't assert that your grandmother's lasagna was the most savory meal ever served, show us the lasagna, layer by layer, and let us smell the tomato sauce, see the flecks of oregano in the ricotta cheese. More importantly, let us see your grandmother, her eyes, her hands, the stoop of her back, the pattern on her apron, and the days she spent preparing ahead for the holiday meal because she believed, as if it were her religion, that food was love.

- Do your research. Historians can go to the collected papers of famous politicians when they want to re-create the past, but perhaps what you are writing about is so obscure that no one kept a record of any sort. Goodness knows if you are old as me, there are no videotapes of every childhood event, just occasional, out of focus black-and-white photos. But there is still research to be done. First, ask people. If family members are alive, ask them what they remember. Even if the memories seem faulty, they will spur you to remember your own versions. Ask friends from the old neighborhood how they perceived your family. Tell them to be honest. Even if your family no longer owns that small farm out on Butter Churn Road, you can perhaps drive out there, park across the street, and let the contour of the landscape and the placement of the trees jog your memory. Sit a while with those old blurry photographs. The more you remember, you will find out, the more you remember beyond that. Each small memory is a string; pull on it, and something new comes up out of the fabric.

- Neither a hero nor a victim be. If the story you share is all about how wonderful you are, why should the reader believe you? And why, other than self-flattery, are you even exploring it on the page? Likewise, if you are pure victim, the dish towel tossed around by unfair family and fickle fates, then what is there to be learned? In truth, most of us are flawed folks who try our best, and on some days we do pretty darn well. On other days? Well, maybe it is best to just go to sleep and start over tomorrow. The struggle! That's what's interesting.

YOUR MEMOIR ESSAY

Please approach the following prompts as just that—prompts. Consider them in no way prescriptive. In other words, if you read my suggestions here and they point you directly down a path that seems productive, by all means start writing your way down that path. But if, on the other hand, you read my suggestion and think, "Well not exactly. I'd rather write about my mother's paint-by-number hobby than about her cooking," by all means listen to and follow your better instincts. Think of these ideas as potential sparks, and if they light a fire in the dry brush of your imagination, don't try too hard to control where that artistic fire leads:

1. Let us begin with a basic list. Answer the following questions with whatever pops up—a one-word answer, a snippet of memory, a rough scene, a seeming non sequitur. Consider it raw material and set

the list aside, to be consulted often when you are looking for a new project or a new direction:

- What are you most afraid of?
- What as a child did you totally misunderstand, but now as an adult see very differently?
- What secret, big or small, have you still not told your parents?
- When was the first time you betrayed a friend?
- At what moment in your life did you realize that your parents were not perfect? That they could not protect you from all troubles? That sometimes they were scared as well?
- What is the most embarrassing moment of your life that occurred in front of strangers, in a checkout line or an airport, or in a foreign city?
- Do you have spindly toes? Fat thumbs? Or what other part of your body do you obsess over as too small, too large, too round, not round enough, oddly proportioned, or totally dull? This makes for a good essay topic especially if the truth is that only *you* notice this "deficiency," while most objective observers think you are just fine. And isn't that usually the case?
- If you could change your name, first, last, or both names, what would you change to? What would this change represent, actually or symbolically? Why do names matter?

2. Here's another direction: Families and food seem to always contain fascinating stories. Whether your family dinners were extravagant ethnic feasts involving roasted slabs of meat and garlic and fried

delicacies and abundance or whether your mother didn't cook at all and your father made dinner from a box (just add water), somehow the ways in which we shared meals as a family tells volumes about who we were. What do your family mealtime rituals, and favorite dishes, reveal about the deeper patterns of family life and relationship?

3. Or perhaps food is not the trigger here. Maybe you should make a list of the cars your father drove—he always seemed to come home with a new clunker, right? Maybe that list will tell something about the man and his hidden aspirations. Or perhaps the constant remodeling projects your mother undertook show how she was trying to convince the neighbors (and herself) of something she thought vitally important.

4. What was unique about the job your father or mother held, or the way your neighbors earned their living? Remember, if your father was a coal miner, for instance, that probably didn't seem very unique to you, because perhaps every father in your neighborhood worked in the mine, but it *is* unique to the average reader. Consider how little most people really know about what coal miners do when *not* down in the mines, what they tell their children about the work, how they relax on weekends. Did having a father who went deep into the dangerous earth day after day influence your view of the world, or of religion, nature, or work? Maybe your uncle was a cop. Or perhaps your mom awoke every morning at 3 A.M. to work in a bakery. Same

questions apply. Or you had an aunt who was a Catholic nun. None of these family scenarios would seem exceptional to the child at the time, but all of it—if told with detail and honesty—can be fascinating to readers whose lives were very different.

5. Did your younger sister have *petit mal* syndrome? What did it seem like to you, at nine, to have a sister who passed out in church, in school, who dropped to the floor with no warning and turned a frightening shade of gray? Did it affect your parent's marriage? Did it make you grow up too fast, or too slow, or too panicky? Again, maybe it is not *petit mal*, and maybe it's not your sister. Maybe your father had an amputated hand. Maybe your mother was dangerously overweight. Maybe you had allergies that closed your swollen eyes shut for days at a time. The point here is not to ask for sympathy, but rather to give the reader an idea of how one person—you—and one family—yours—coped with circumstances that might be very different or might run rather parallel to the circumstances they themselves faced.

6. What is most peculiar about your character? I mean really peculiar, not the sort of safe peculiar ("Oh, I simply go crazy when I see chocolate!") details we easily share with strangers. Maybe as a child you collected rodent skeletons, or maybe today you have a kitchen drawer containing over one thousand grocery store twisty ties. Do you still have an imaginary friend, one to whom you confess your secrets, even though you are thirty-four-years old?

Do you have elaborate daydreams about under-water lands in which you are an elusive mermaid, and you've been constructing this mental fantasy for over a decade? Do you compulsively steal (well, they are technically free) mustard packets from fast-food restaurants? Come on, be honest. Every-one has a hidden quirk. The interesting question here is why? What is the attraction?

7. Choose a family memory that everyone seems to remember differently. Now explore. Tell us your ver-sion. Tell us your sister's version. Tell us how your mother remembers it, or that she refuses to remem-ber it all. ("Oh, that never happened, dear!") Don't try to win the argument, or to prove your memory surer than others, but instead explore the gap. Why might everyone in your family want to remember this Christmas Eve a bit differently? What does each version tell us about the unspoken family hierarchy? Does it matter who is right and who is wrong, or are you all right in your own way?

8. What have you forgotten? This may seem like an odd prompt, but often what is absent from our memory tells a story as well. Summer camp? The year your parents almost divorced? Your broken arm? What might be the truth about that missing gap? What can you learn by asking others, and what will you never know?

9. Music! My older sisters blasted the Rolling Stones and some British pop group named after an insect when I was eight, but I wanted so much to own a forty-five of the Royal Guardsmen's "Snoopy vs.

The Red Baron." My mother would tear up at almost any Sinatra tune, while my father, to the best of my knowledge, never purchased music, attended a concert, or turned on the radio in his life. He did, however, love the comedy albums of George Carlin. Is there an interesting memoir essay here? I don't know. And I'll never know, unless I start *assaying*—trying out my memories and ideas to see where they lead.

THE WOOLF AND
THE MOTH

"The style of the essayist is that of an extremely intelligent, highly commonsensical person talking, without stammer and with impressive coherence, to him—or herself and to anyone else who cares to eavesdrop."
—Joseph Epstein

Michel de Montaigne was as peculiar a fellow as you could ever hope to meet. He was born at his family estate in Château de Montaigne, in southwest France, heir to a herring merchant's fish-scented fortune. His father harbored some "modern" ideas about education, however, so as a baby Montaigne was sent to live the first three years of life in the sole company of a peasant family.

Later, when the boy returned to the Château, his father hired only servants who were fluent in Latin, and instructed them to speak exclusively in the classic language when in young Michel's presence. A zither player was hired to follow the boy and play a tune any time Montaigne became bored or tired.

I'm not making this up.

The idea was for the young Frenchman to fully appreciate classical thought and music while still having absorbed the lessons of a humble beginning, and for the young boy to become an intellectual of great distinction.

It worked.

In 1571, at the age of thirty-eight, Montaigne gave up his career in law and government service, and retired, as he put it, "to the bosom of the learned virgins." Back at the Château, he began his *Essais*, a series of personal ruminations on topics as diverse as idleness, body odor, and cannibals, and along the way he changed the course of literature.

Some will argue that Montaigne's new essay form merely mimicked a tradition that goes back to Greek and Roman orators, but that's an academic argument, and one we needn't concern ourselves with here. Unquestionably, the herring merchant's grandson put his firm stamp on personal writing—in fact, made writing about the self possible—and inspired British authors such as William Hazlitt, Charles Lamb, and Thomas De Quincey to follow his lead.

I recommend checking in with Montaigne's essays: They are odd, humorous, quite radical for their times, and no matter what your writing genre—poetry, the novel, even cookbooks—it is always a good thing to understand the tradition you hope to join.

But by all means, remember that it is *not* your goal to mimic Montaigne's archaic diction or his penchant for Greek and Latin references. You are writing in the twenty-first century, so find your twenty-first-century voice.

As Hazlitt instructed, "To write a genuine familiar or truly English style is to write as any one would speak in common conversation who had a thorough command of and choice of words, who could discourse with ease, force, and perspicuity, setting aside all pedantic and oratorical flourishes."

Now maybe Hazlitt's words seem themselves dense and pedantic, but that's exactly the point. Styles change. Serious readers in the sixteenth and eighteenth centuries were very different than the contemporary audience for nonfiction, and trying to write in the tone or style of a literary masterpiece won't make your work a masterpiece as well. Instead, it will most likely make your work seem peculiar, out-of-date, and will offer an uncomfortable reading experience for those who prefer to be spoken to directly.

Thus ends our brief lesson in the history of the essay. It does well to know what came before you, but write for tomorrow, not for the past.

WRITING EXERCISE: LEARNING FROM THE MASTER

Take this opening paragraph from one of the early essays of Michael de Montaigne, and attempt to translate it into twenty-first century common speech.

Here's Montaigne's version, from his essay "Of Repentance":

> Others form man; I only report him: and represent a particular one, ill fashioned enough, and whom, if I had to model him anew, I should certainly make something else than what he is: but that's past recalling. Now, though the features of my picture alter and change, 'tis not, however, unlike: the world eternally turns round; all things therein are incessantly moving, the earth, the rocks of Caucasus, and the pyramids of Egypt, both by the public motion and their own. Even constancy itself is no

other but a slower and more languishing motion. I cannot fix my object; 'tis always tottering and reeling by a natural giddiness: I take it as it is at the instant I consider it; I do not paint its being, I paint its passage; not a passing from one age to another, or, as the people say, from seven to seven years, but from day to day, from minute to minute.

Now that's a mouthful, certainly, but essentially Montaigne is telling the reader that he, the author, is constantly changing, and warning the same reader that any picture Montaigne presents of himself is just a moment in time.

Can you convey the same ideas, in the sort of language you might use to speak with a dear friend?

In this chapter's epigraph, Joseph Epstein suggests that an essayist should attempt to capture the voice of "an extremely intelligent, highly commonsensical person talking, without stammer and with impressive coherence." Let that be your target: everyday speech, but with the stammering removed, and the coherence turned up just a notch. That's the true beauty of writing after all—we can have a good idea, and then revise it to sound even better, and then clear away the brush to make it stand out in the open field.

WRITING THE CLASSIC (BUT NEVER MOLDY) ESSAY

Despite eccentricities of language and style, we can learn from Montaigne the basic essay impulse: to ruminate, consider, explore. The writer of a personal essay does not begin with an idea and then struggle to prove her point; she investigates, keeps an open mind, goes wherever the thought may lead, and, in fact, may end the essay having still not reached a final conclusion.

"My conceptions and my judgment move only by groping, staggering, stumbling, and blundering," Montaigne wrote, "and when I have gone ahead as far as I can, still I am not at all satisfied."

Virginia Woolf, one of the foremost literary figures of the twentieth century, wrote novels and essays alike, and she understood the impulse to explore in writing, rather than to lecture.

A careful look at her classic work "The Death of the Moth" shows how a small event can expand outward, moment by moment, until the whole is so much greater than the sum of the parts. The "theme" of Woolf's essay—mortality as a constant and inevitable presence in the natural world—is common enough, but Woolf brings us an intimate and highly personal view.

By the way, I put the word theme in quotation marks above because it is always a mistake to oversimplify the mysterious soul that burrows deep in the center of any successful writing. If the point of a work of art could be reduced to one word or a short phrase—"man's inhumanity to man," for instance—well, then we'd need only to write that word or phrase on an index card and be done with it.

Of course, that is not the case. Woolf's essay is "about" the inevitability of death, certainly, but it's filled with many strong undercurrents. With each new reading, a fresh angle on the subject seems to present itself.

So, with that in mind, on to the suggestions.

The World in a Small Thing

Woolf opens her essay "The Death of the Moth" simply enough, with a consideration of the sorts of moths that fly through the English countryside. Quickly though, her focus turns to a single insect, a daytime moth with "narrow hay-coloured wings, fringed with a tassel of the same colour." She suggests that this moth, seen on her windowsill, "seemed to be content with life," and a careful reader might interpret this as a window into Woolf's own mood that morning. When we are content, the whole world somehow seems contented. When we are anxious or unhappy, we see the unsettledness in all people and all things.

Woolf quite deliberately employs one of the most effective ways of anchoring a reader into an essay. She chooses something small, tangible, something with which we are all familiar, as her initial subject. "Sure," the reader thinks, "I've seen moths around my house in September. That's when they start coming inside, looking for warmth."

Imagine if instead Woolf had begun her essay with gloomy pronouncements about death being inevitable. "No matter what happens," she might have written, "death will find you, and we will all end up buried below the deep, deep earth."

Well, we know that to be true, but most of us are not so eager to plunge right into the thought, are we?

The Power of Metaphor

Woolf's entire essay is just under 1,200 words, so she wastes no time on fluff or repetition. In a sentence or two, she turns her observation to the view of the English countryside out the window on which the moth has settled, and then she soon enough begins the exploration that marks the "trying out" that is at the heart of every successful *assay*.

Woolf watches the moth fluttering on the windowpane awhile, wondering at the moth's persistence, but also at the sad lot of an insect who had few other choices but to beat against the glass of the window. Soon she offers this passage:

> Watching him, it seemed as if a fibre, very thin but pure, of the enormous energy of the world had been thrust into his frail and diminutive body ... as if someone had taken a tiny bead of pure life and ... had set it dancing and zig-zagging ...

Orson Scott Card, the celebrated science fiction author, reminds us that "metaphors have a way of holding the most truth in the least space," and Woolf has seamlessly let the moth become metaphor.

Now the essay is about so much more than just that sad insect on the window.

 ## WRITING EXERCISE: WHAT'S A METAPHOR?

Look around you, at the objects in your office, the food in your kitchen, the plants, animals, and insects outside your back door, or at the busy chaos of urban life outside of your apartment window, and think of what you see beyond the literal.

You will need to take you fingers off this book and step away from your keyboard for this to happen. You will need to slow down, stroll around, and just wait for something to suggest itself. You will probably want to force a metaphor, and you might even get anxious when nothing comes in the first five minutes, but make a cup of tea, find a comfortable place to sit where you can see a wide vista, and just look at everything with close attention.

Say to yourself, "Gee, that (fill in the blank) also reminds me of (fill in the blank)," and be ready to discard your first thirty or forty notions. Really, do it fast, and understand that in most cases the metaphor will seem strained and too thin to explore. Run through them like a bowl of potato chips.

But when one finally hits the target, when it seems natural and makes sense even when you go back to it a third time, then start writing. Just see where it leads.

What's a metaphor?

It's for spurring us along so that we might see the world in new ways.

Actions Speak Loudly

You've likely heard the saying "Actions speak louder than words" about four thousand times in your life. Every once in a while I bristle at the thought. Wait, I think, words are powerful, too. Certain books—consisting of nothing *but* words—have changed history, moved entire nations to reconsider slavery or war or class oppression.

But still, I understand the central idea behind the oft-repeated aphorism. Talk is cheap. If you want to truly know someone's character, watch what they actually do (good or bad, selfish or selfless), and weigh that against the cloud of words they spew into the air. Suppose the neighbor to your left has a "Love thy neighbor" bumper sticker prominently displayed on the back of his car, while the neighbor to your right crosses the street twice a month and mows the lawn for the elderly woman who can no longer do it herself? Who do you believe?

Novelists know that this rule is also an important part of building character. A writer can tell you over and over that Mrs. Wimple is a kindhearted soul, but it is not until the reader sees her acting in a kindhearted way on the page that the impression is solidly established. Or think of the hypocritical blowhards in those wonderful Charles Dickens' novels, portrayed as saying one thing repeatedly while always doing the other.

Action (captured in words) is a powerful tool for nonfiction writers as well.

For instance, there is more than just a moth in that room where Virginia Woolf reads and writes; there is a human being, Woolf herself, and she knows that the reader is going to most directly experience this moment by seeing it through another human being's eyes.

So Woolf describes in great detail how her eyes were caught by the moth's initial movements, how she had trouble focusing on the work before her because she kept looking up at the moth's increasingly weak attempts, and how she eventually found herself distracted even when the moth was still, because she was waiting for the next flutter.

And then she finally takes an action. In her essay, she reaches over for a pencil, considers helping the moth to right itself on the window ledge, and then thinks again, and puts the pencil back down.

Now that's not much. She picks up her pencil, almost acts, but in the end thinks better of it. Hmm, why so little?

Well, first off, this is nonfiction, so Woolf is telling us the truth. She reached for that pencil, and then she hesitated. That's what happened, so that's what she tells us.

But remembering the metaphor Woolf has carefully constructed, making the moth more than just a creature with "narrow hay-coloured" wings, is she maybe telling us something else as well?

The Moth Matters

At any point in Woolf's brief essay, she could easily have veered off into the abstractions of her subject. Death is after all an area of human existence that often leads to sermonizing and philosophical bromides. A less experienced writer might have succumbed to the temptation, but Woolf is keenly aware of her reader, and the need for the reader to remain grounded not just in idea but in story.

So Woolf returns again and again to the actual, physical moth that appeared in her study on that mid-September day, and she even gives him (Woolf decided the moth was masculine, though in truth I suppose she was guessing) the last word:

> The moth having righted himself now lay most
> decently and uncomplainingly composed. O yes,
> he seemed to say, death is stronger than I am.

Her syntax at the end is a bit formal, at least to my modern ears, but remember that she wrote this essay in 1942.

There is so much to be learned from this brief, classic essay. The moth is dead, and there is nothing Woolf can do about it, just as there is nothing she can do about what she observes out her window in mid-September, the natural change of autumn which inevitably leads to winter, and the cycle of nature which is, most certainly, stronger than all of us.

MY ASSAY: WHEREIN THE AUTHOR ATTEMPTS TO FOLLOW HIS OWN ADVICE

What does Virginia Woolf teach me that might be helpful as I draft my own essay, "On Foot"?

Well, for one she has reminded me to move briskly away from my general pronouncements on Boca as a beachfront paradise and get down to the physical world. Actions speak louder than words, so if my essay is about my enjoyment of walking, I had better establish that this is true.

Here is what I'm considering putting in right after my introduction:

> "I enjoy a good walk," I insisted when a graduate student named Nicole offered to pick me up from my hotel lobby each day and deliver me directly to campus. "It's only about a mile, right?"
>
> "But I'm *happy* to pick you up," Nicole repeated but I simply didn't catch what she was attempting to tell me at the time.
>
> "I'll be fine," I offered breezily. "Just fine."

But those are just words, of course, so then this:

> The simple mile, a mere stroll for someone who enjoys walking as much as I enjoy walking, ran almost entirely along Glades Road, a six-lane highway whose main purpose, it turns out, is to funnel thousands of automobiles every fifteen minutes or so onto, off of, and over I-95.
>
> At the point that I-95 passes through the heart of Boca, the interstate has ten lanes, so for most of my walk that Monday morning I was dodging

entrance ramps, exit ramps, and scores of impatient
drivers scowling behind tinted windows because
I hadn't enough sense to find a proper, wheeled
vehicle, was just slowing everything down.

Still, I plunged forward, across the concrete-
circles-of-hell, toward what the map told me
would be the entrance to the FAU campus.

As you may have guessed already, my experience walking
through Boca Raton just got worse and worse as my week-
long visit went on. But the essay can't be just about me or just
about my complaints. I need to discover my larger point.

So far, all I have is this metaphor forming in my mind.
Boca Raton is a wealthy community, full of gated estates,
luxury high-rise condos, and mansions that appear vacant
because the shutters and windows are perpetually closed
to keep out the blazing sun. Despite all of the cars whizzing here and there along the main highways and secondary arteries, the town itself can feel pretty empty, as if the
drivers are just passing through to another destination. I
walked and walked through that town, all the way to the
beach, and barely saw another soul, other than those in
the automobiles.

The fact that no one seemed out and about, strolling
along the sidewalks, working in their yards, throwing Frisbees, or walking their dogs, combined with the grand homes
all shuttered up, air-conditioned, and set off by fences and
gates, made me think of mausoleums, or Egyptian pyramids.
It seemed almost as if these wealthy folks were already entombed, just waiting for their deaths.

Maybe Woolf has influenced me here, too. My essay is starting to feel pretty gloomy. I'll have to give that some thought,
since my intention is not to bore or depress the reader.

In any case, I'm not yet sure if this metaphor will pan out, or how the various pieces now fit together. I just have to keep writing to see where it leads.

ON THE IMPORTANCE OF FEARLESSNESS

Essayist Nancy Mairs has written, "It's as though some writers have the sense never to enter the room until they've thrown the switch and flooded it with light, whereas others, like me, insist on entering rooms with burnt-out bulbs or blown fuses or no wiring at all."

There is great wisdom in her words. Michel de Montaigne may have been an odd man, but he was fearless about his writing and entered many dark rooms with no wiring yet installed. He went so far as to invent a new form, he tackled subjects others felt not worthy of literature, and he carved out a place for the I in the essay, insisting that his opinions mattered and making room for those who followed.

I'm still not sure why his father thought it a good idea to hire a zither player to follow young Michel around the family's lofty estate, but all in all, I'm glad that he did.

WRITING THE
CONTEMPLATIVE ESSAY

*"If you can speak what you will never hear, if you
can write what you will never read, you have
done rare things."*
—Henry David Thoreau

I can remember as a young man dreaming that someday
I would be a writer. My dreams included my byline in a
magazine, my picture on the "featured contributors" page,
and eventually my name on the cover of a book. On days
that I let my dreams run wild and free, I fantasized about
hefty royalty checks and a cozy house on the rocky coast
of Maine.

Well, some of this has come true (after thirty years of
stubborn progress), and some of it has not (in truth, I've
yet to even visit Maine), but what I *have* learned along the
way is that my dreams were missing the point entirely. The
rewards of publication are fleeting, while the rewards of a
regular writing practice are countless.

You may have run across the famous quote from essayist Joan Didion: "I write to find out what I'm thinking,
what I'm looking at, what I see, and what it means." Or perhaps this one from Jean Malaquais: "The only time I know

that something is true is the moment I discover it in the act of writing."

Accomplished authors often comment on the idea that they have little or no sureness of what they want to say until they've actually put it down on the page.

Why is this notion so popular?

Because it is true. And this self-knowledge is the true prize for the writer.

As Didion and Malaquais have realized, the happy by-product of arranging the perfect sentences in the exact order necessary, of capturing in language those moments that most people simply dismiss as being "too hard to put into words," is that one has a richer life. Knowing what we think, see, feel, and what it all may mean to us beyond the current moment leads inevitably to a deeper appreciation of all that surrounds us, both the joys *and* the challenges.

As Heraclitus reportedly once advised, "Know thyself!"

Which brings us to the contemplative essay.

Best-selling novelist Ann Patchett once said, "Writing is a job, a talent, but it's also the place to go in your head. It is the imaginary friend you drink your tea with in the afternoon," and the contemplative essay is what you might share with that friend.

In fact, some believe the essay form as devised by Montaigne came about because of the grief he felt when his close friend, the poet Étienne de la Boétie, died young. Montaigne's essays were the conversations he would have shared with his dear friend, had de la Boétie lived.

Of course, writing is always a bit artificial, and I mean that in a good way. When I try to explain a complex thought process to my friends at the dinner table, I usually stammer, stumble, contradict myself, lose my way, and follow numerous inefficient paths back to my main point. When I write an essay, I have the luxury of editing, and rethinking, and rearranging, so that—on a good day—a reader thinks, "My, that Moore fellow sure thinks clearly."

It is an illusion, of course. Just like the finest ballet dancer makes that leap into the air seem so effortless and natural only after hours upon hours of painful, strenuous studio work, the better writers seem naturally articulate on the page even though their first drafts may have been total, muddled wrecks.

So the contemplative essay combines the sense of free-form thinking with careful editing to create the artifice of good conversation on the page. Of course, you can't have actual conversation, unless you are coauthoring with another person, so it falls upon you to hold up both ends.

Ask questions.

Suggest alternative ways of looking at things.

That's what the contemplative essay is all about.

A Note on Meandering

One of the pleasures of the contemplative essay, for the reader, is the meandering sense of the form, the idea that you are taking a leisurely stroll with an interesting mind. It is lovely to observe the author as he glides off on an unexpected tangent, presents a few loop-the-loops, or does some graceful wing tilt, before he glides effortlessly home.

But this too is an illusion of sorts.

The personal essay can seem as if the author is just ambling along, considering various thought flowers along the winding path, but remember that the writer has to be in control (by the later drafts, not necessarily at the beginning).

And remember the reader, always.

"A responsibility of literature is to make people awake, present, alive," Natalie Goldberg advises. "If the writer wanders, then the reader, too, will wander. The fly on the table might be part of the whole description of a restaurant. It might be appropriate to tell precisely the sandwich that it just walked over, but there is a fine line between precision and self-indulgence."

Even the most contemplative, wide-ranging essay is telling a story of sorts, and the reader is on a quest to see how all of the pieces will add up.

So always ask yourself as a writer, "Is this piece a piece of the larger story, or am I just wandering off the track?"

Three Quick Tips

- The best areas to explore in writing are those areas that you truly don't understand. If you already firmly believe that something is wrong, then you will discover very little putting your convictions into an essay. (Write a letter to the editor instead.) If you know that you are entirely in favor of something, then why put forth the effort to dissect and explore? But certain situations—those gray areas of human existence—seem never to resolve themselves. For instance, why do two essentially good people who try hard to make a marriage work still sometimes fail? Are children better off with two parents who remain married but are always tense and at the edge of anger, or are they better off with two divorced parents, shuffling from household to household? Are there victimless crimes, and if so, why does the government spend time and resources enforcing laws against them? These questions never seem easily answered, especially when they involve people you know and love.

- Before writing, make a list of all of the common points—the clichés and usual turns of discussion—around the topic you are exploring. Then write an essay using none of those common points.

- Tackle something so vexing that in the end you wind up surprising yourself.

YOUR CONTEMPLATIVE ESSAY

Please recall my admonition from a few chapters back—the following prompts are in no way prescriptive but instead are designed to point you in a direction. If that direction leads somewhere fruitful, then by all means go ahead and follow where I have pointed. If you feel pulled in a contradictory direction, however, give in to that urge. The goal here is not to win a "most cooperative student" star on your report card; the goal is to be writing in a fresh and surprising way.

1. Consider this peculiar passage from our role model Montaigne: "'Tis not to be believed how strangely all sorts of odours cleave to me, and how apt my skin is to imbibe them. He that complains of nature that she has not furnished mankind with a vehicle to convey smells to the nose had no reason; for they will do it themselves, especially to me; my very mustachios, which are full, perform that office; for if I stroke them but with my gloves or handkerchief, the smell will not out a whole day; they manifest where I have been ..." Now, don't let the fancy words fool you. What he is saying is that if he eats a corned beef and rye for lunch, with mustard, he can still smell it on his whiskers at

bed time. Montaigne was all about his own peculiarities, and he was never shy about sharing. What are your foibles and peculiarities? You might begin with a list, but eventually choose one—the odder the better, but pick one you aren't too ashamed to discuss freely—and try to bring the reader into your confidence.

2. Here's Montaigne again: "Others shape the man; I portray him, and offer to the view one in particular, who is ill-shaped enough, and whom, could I refashion him, I should certainly make very different from what he is." This was, in truth, a radical notion at the time. Writers were supposed to portray noble virtues and draw straight lines signifying the path to righteousness. Montaigne would have none of that. He believed in portraying the truth about himself, his "ill-shaped" nature, and if you've read much recent memoir, you know that Montaigne started a movement that continues even today. So who are you, really? What makes you human?

3. Another classic essayist, William Hazlitt, began an essay thusly: "One of the pleasantest things in the world is going a journey; but I like to go by myself. I can enjoy society in a room; but out of doors, nature is company enough for me. I am then never less alone than when alone." Do you prefer traveling alone or with company? Contemplate for a moment how the experience of walking through deep woods feels when you are simply by yourself and how it feels when you are in the company of a congenial friend. (Better yet, find a forest or

lakeside and actually have the experience before writing.) How about a museum or historic cathedral? Do you crave solitude when in the presence of art and architecture, or good company?

4. Hazlitt's contemporary, Charles Lamb, writes that "The human species, according to the best theory I can form of it, is composed of two distinct races, the men who borrow, and the men who lend." Now that's an interesting dichotomy, but certainly we could divide the human race up in any number of thousands of way. People who eat fast food while driving home from the drive-through and those who would never be caught dead with mustard streaming down the front of their shirt. People who floss every night and those who do not. People who buy more books than they can ever read and people who haven't held a book since high school. Those who are publicly religious and those who keep their spiritual beliefs deeply hidden. What dichotomy makes sense to you? Explore.

5. Woolf observed the finality of death by watching that ill-fated moth, but others of us realize this in other ways: the death of a parent, the withering of a summer garden, the site of a dead fawn in the forest. Where have you encountered death, and other than the obvious emotions of sadness and loss, what was evoked?

6. What has changed about modern manners and customs, such as the holding of doors for women, respect for the elderly, kindness to strangers,

behavior at four-way stop signs. Avoid merely sounding cranky here, however. What is lost when certain customs fade away, and why does it matter?

7. You can, of course, take the alternate view, that certain customs that have faded away are gone for good reason, and we are all better off.

8. Why do so many of our politicians, especially the ones who are so quick to tell us what *our* moral values should be, end up involved in their own marital sex scandals? Don't waste time decrying the fact: After all, there are few enough people out there who think sex scandals are a *good* thing. Instead, consider what it is about human nature that makes this so.

9. What are the traits that identify a quality next-door neighbor? Are those traits lost or just refashioned in the modern world?

10. We all, as Walt Whitman once pointed out, contain multitudes. Write an essay from the point-of-view of your *hopeful* self. In what ways can you suggest that the world is not going to hell in a hand basket, that climate change is not about to destroy us all, that human civilization is not spiraling into a narcissistic void?

11. Write an essay titled "In Praise of *Not* Walking in the Woods."

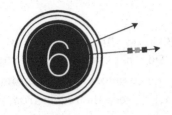

A CLOSER LOOK: "LEISURE"

BY AGNES REPPLIER

The contemplative essay is progenitor of the entire creative nonfiction form, the "Adam and Eve of the Essay," you might say. Though styles and tastes have changed over the centuries, those early essays—St. Augustine, Montaigne, Bacon—form the basis for what we now call memoir, literary journalism, the lyric essay, and the personal essay. They inform travel writing, nature writing, spiritual writing, and scientific writing. Perhaps the best way to fully understand how this form took shape in these earlier centuries, and how vestiges of the form remain alive in the contemporary essay of today, is to look closely at a full example.

The essay "Leisure" by Agnes Repplier was first published in 1893, and as I've warned in previous chapters, it does sound a little "overwritten" to the twenty-first-century ear. The diction is heightened, and many of the sentences seem unusually long.

To be entirely honest, many of the essays I read from the nineteenth, eighteenth, or seventeenth centuries just seem way too long for me. I'm an impatient reader. When I'm working with a beginning writer, my most frequent suggestion probably goes like this: "You don't get to your point until page three! Do you expect the reader to venture three pages into your piece before understanding what this essay is about? What's to keep the reader from paging ahead in the magazine and finding something else to read?"

But to complain too much about the length or weighty diction or ruminative pace of these essays of an earlier century is like complaining that Shakespeare wrote in an odd language—he *did*, because that was the language of his time and it only sounds odd to us—or that we don't like the paintings of Caravaggio so much because everyone is wearing such old-fashioned clothes.

Well, that's just silly, right?

Truth is, there was a time, back before e-mail, before television, before automobiles, that folks had very little to entertain or distract them, at least those folks who made up the educated, literate classes, and when these folks sat down with a magazine or book, they didn't want the experience to go quickly. They wanted it to fill the evening. The result: longer essays, with thoughts and ideas drawn out like taffy, stretched to the seeming limit.

Once you know what these writers are up to in their essays, it becomes easier to appreciate the work that they did, even if you end up preferring more contemporary work.

Let me introduce Agnes Repplier, the woman and writer, and then we will commence with her essay.

Repplier, born in 1855, began writing as a young woman, first for *Catholic World*, a magazine published by the Paulist Fathers, and eventually for more mainstream magazines such as *The Atlantic Monthly, The New Republic, McClure's,* and *Harper's.* She was able to earn a decent living from her writing and speaking engagements, enough to eventually travel widely. She authored roughly two dozen books over her life and reached the age of ninety-five.

Like her forerunner Montaigne often chose to do, Repplier begins her essay with a quotation—*"Zounds! how has he the leisure to be sick?"* A contemporary writer would be expected to reveal the source of such a quote, but expectations were different in 1893: The literary canon was made up of fewer works, a liberal education was focused keenly on "great books," and many in Repplier's readership would recognize instantly that this quote comes from Shakespeare's *King Henry IV, Part 1.*

Employing another move common to essayists of her time, Repplier begins "Leisure" not with her own opinions or observations, but by considering what some other writers and thinkers—Voltaire and Dickens—had to say on her subject.

LEISURE BY AGNES REPPLIER

"Zounds! how has he the leisure to be sick?"

A visitor strolling through the noble woods of Ferney complimented Voltaire on the splendid growth of his trees. "Ay," replied the great wit, half in scorn and half, perhaps, in envy, "they have nothing else to do;" and walked on, deigning no further word of approbation.

Has it been more than a hundred years since this distinctly modern sentiment was uttered, more than a hundred years since the spreading chestnut boughs bent kindly over the lean, strenuous, caustic, disappointed man of genius who always had so much to do, and who found in the doing of it a mingled bliss and bitterness that scorched him like fever pain? How is it that, while Dr. Johnson's sledge-hammer repartees sound like the sonorous echoes of a past age, Voltaire's remarks always appear to have been spoken the day before yesterday? They are the kind of witticisms which we do not say for ourselves, simply because we are not witty; but they illustrate with biting accuracy the spirit of restlessness, of disquiet, of intellectual vanity and keen contention which is the brand of our vehement and over-zealous generation.

"The Gospel of Work"—that is the phrase woven insistently into every homily, every appeal made to the conscience or the intelligence of a people who are now straining their youthful energy to its utmost speed. "Blessed be Drudgery!" that is the text deliberately chosen for a discourse which has enjoyed such amazing popularity that sixty thousand printed copies have been found all inadequate to supply the ravenous demand. Readers of Dickens if anyone has the time to read Dickens nowadays may remember Miss Monflather's inspired amendment of that familiar poem concerning the Busy Bee:

In work, work, work. In work always,
Let my first years be past.

And when our first years are past, the same programme is considered adequate and satisfactory to the end. "A whole lifetime of horrid industry," to quote Mr. Bagehot's uninspired words, this is the prize dangled alluringly before our tired eyes; and if we are disposed to look askance upon the booty, then vanity is subtly pricked to give zest to faltering resolution. "Our virtues would be proud if our faults whipped them not;" they would be laggards in the field if our faults did not sometimes spur them to action. It is the paean of self-glorification that wells up perpetually from press and pulpit, from public orators, and from what is courteously called literature, that keeps our courage screwed to the sticking place, and veils the occasional bareness of the result with a charitable vesture of self-delusion.

Work is good. No one seriously doubts this truth. Adam may have doubted it when he first took spade in hand, and Eve when she scoured her first pots and kettles; but in the course of a few thousand years we have learned to know and value this honest, troublesome, faithful, and extremely exacting friend. But work is not the only good thing in the world; it is not a fetish to be adored; neither is it to be judged, like a sum in addition, by its outward and immediate results. The god of labor does not abide exclusively in the rolling-mill, the law courts, or the corn field. He has a twin sister whose name is leisure, and in her society he lingers now and then to the lasting gain of both.

LET ME INTERRUPT, if you will, for just a bit of translation and analysis.

Repplier begins her contemplative essay, like many public speakers still do today, with a joke, or at the very least, a light moment—Voltaire's offhand witticism about the trees—but quickly begins to hint at her true subject, dropping in phrases such as "our vehement and over-zealous generation" and "a whole lifetime of horrid industry." Soon enough she is decrying those who preach the "gospel of work," and asking if they are perhaps misguided in their zealous promotion of hard, ceaseless labor.

She is engaging in social criticism, questioning the values of the society in which she finds herself, and though it takes a while, she finally, in the paragraph that begins "Work is good," reaches her primary point, or thesis: Work is not "the only good thing," but "has a twin sister, whose name is leisure, and in her society he lingers now and then to the lasting gain of both." Or in other words, a bit of balance is a good thing.

She goes on to explore concepts of leisure, using the example of Mme. de Sévigné, a seventeenth-century

French aristocrat known for her witty and vivid letter writing, and Montaigne himself, to reinforce her points:

Sainte-Beuve, writing of Mme. de Sévigné and her time, says that we, "with our habits of positive occupation, can scarcely form a just conception of that life of leisure and chit-chat." "Conversations were infinite," admits Mme. de Sévigné herself, recalling the long summer afternoons when she and her guests walked in the charming woods of Les Rochers until the shadows of twilight fell. The whole duty of life seemed to be concentrated in the pleasant task of entertaining your friends when they were with you, or writing them admirable letters when they were absent. Occasionally there came, even to this tranquil and finely poised French woman, a haunting consciousness that there might be other and harder work for human hands to do. "Nothing is accomplished day by day," she writes, doubtfully; "and life is made up of days, and we grow old and die." This troubled her a little, when she was all the while doing work that was to last for generations, work that was to give pleasure to men and women whose great-grandfathers were then unborn. Not that we have the time now to read Mme. de Sévigné! Why, there are big volumes of these delightful letters, and who can afford to read big volumes of anything, merely for the sake of the enjoyment to be extracted there from? It was all very well for Sainte-Beuve to say *Lisonstout Mme. de Sévigné,* when the question arose how should some long idle days in a country-house be profitably employed. It was all very well for Sainte-Beuve to plead, with touching confidence in the intellectual pastimes of his contemporaries, "Let us treat Mme. de Sévigné as we treat Clarissa Harlowe, when we have a fortnight of leisure and rainy weather in the country." A fortnight of leisure and rainy weather in the country! The words would be antiquated even for Dr. Johnson. Rain may fall or rain may cease, but leisure comes not so lightly to our calling. Nay, Sainte-Beuve's wistful amazement at the polished and cultivated inactivity which alone could produce such a correspondence as Mme. de Sévigné's is not greater than our wistful amazement at the critic's conception of possible idleness in bad weather. In one respect at least we follow his good counsel. We do treat Mme. de Sévigné precisely as we treat Clarissa Harlowe; that is, we leave them both severely alone, as being utterly beyond the reach of what we are pleased to call our time.

And what of the leisure of Montaigne, who, taking his life in his two hands, disposed of it as he thought fit, with no restless self-accusations on the score of indolence. In the world and of the world, yet always able to meet and greet the happy solitude of Gascony; toiling with no thought of toil, but rather "to entertain my spirit as it best pleased," this man wrought out of time a coin which passes current over the reading world. And what of Horace, who enjoyed an industrious idleness, the bare description of which sets our hearts aching with desire! "The picture which Horace draws of himself in his country home," says an envious English critic, "affords us a delightful glimpse of such literary leisure as is only possible in the golden days of good Haroun-Al-Kaschid. Horace goes to bed and gets up when he likes; there is no one to drag him down to the law courts the first thing in the morning, to remind him of an important engagement with his brother scribes, to solicit his interest with Maecenas, or to tease him about public affairs and the latest news from abroad. He can bury himself in his Greek authors, or ramble through the woody glens which lie at the foot of Mount Ustica, without a thought of business or a feeling that he ought to be otherwise engaged."

"Swim smoothly in the stream of thy nature, and live but one man," counsels Sir Thomas Browne; and it may be this gentle current will bear us as bravely through life as if we buffeted our strength away in the restless ocean of endeavor.

AS I MENTIONED at the outset, the contemporary reader might have a hard time with some of Repplier's dated references, and with the denseness of her prose, but slow down the pace of your reading a bit and you will notice some very lovely turns of phrases and images.

Now that she has established (with the help of Voltaire, Dickens, Montaigne, etcetera) the importance of leisure to the human soul and intellect, she is about to make a turn in her essay. Leisure, she says in the first paragraph below, is not only of utmost importance to the individual, something they should "know how to cultivate, to use, and to enjoy," but leisure also "has a distinct and honorable place" in society, especially a progressive society where the citizenry "are released from the pressure of their first rude needs, their first homely toil ..."

She goes even a step further, quoting one of her contemporaries, Henry Blake Fuller, who asserted that "the success of any society worth considering is to be estimated largely by the use to which its *fortunati*—those fortunate enough to have leisure time—"put their spare moments."

Or to paraphrase: Americans are too enamored with hard work, to the exclusion of relaxation and leisurely contemplation, and in Repplier's opinion, that is not the mark of superior nation or civilization.

Leisure has a value of its own. It is not a mere handmaid of labor; it is something we should know how to cultivate, to use, and to enjoy. It has a distinct and honorable place wherever nations are released from the pressure of their first rude needs, their first homely toil, and rise to happier levels of grace and intellectual repose. "Civilization, in its final outcome," says the keen young author of *The*

Crafting the Personal Essay

Chevalier of Pensieri-Vani, "is heavily in the debt of leisure; and the success of any society worth considering is to be estimated largely by the use to which its *fortunati* put their spare moments." Here is a sentiment so relentlessly true that nobody wants to believe it. We prefer uttering agreeable platitudes concerning the blessedness of drudgery and the iniquity of eating bread earned by another's hands. Yet the creation of an artistic and intellectual atmosphere in which workers can work, the expansion of a noble sympathy with all that is finest and most beautiful, the jealous guardianship of whatever makes the glory and distinction of a nation; this is achievement enough for the *fortunati* of any land, and this is the debt they owe. It can hardly be denied that the lack of scholarship, of classical scholarship especially, at our universities is due primarily to the labor-worship which is the prevalent superstition of our day, and which, like all superstitions, has gradually degraded its god into an idol, and lost sight of the higher powers and attributes beyond. The student who is pleased to think a knowledge of German "more useful" than a knowledge of Greek; the parent who deliberately declares that his boys have "no time to waste" over Homer; the man who closes the doors of his mind to everything that does not bear directly on mathematics, or chemistry, or engineering, or whatever he calls "work;" all these plead in excuse the exigencies of life, the absolute and imperative necessity of labor.

It would appear, then, that we have no *fortunati*, that we are not yet rich enough to afford the greatest of all luxuries leisure to cultivate and enjoy "the best that has been known and thought in the world." This is a pity, because there seems to be money in plenty for so many less valuable things. The yearly taxes of the United States sound to innocent ears like the fabled wealth of the Orient; the yearly expenditures of the people are on no rigid scale; yet we are too poor to harbor the priceless literature of the past because it is not a paying investment, because it will not put bread in our mouths nor clothes on our shivering nakedness. "Poverty is a most odious calling," sighed Burton many years ago, and we have good cause to echo his lament. Until we are able to believe, with that enthusiastic Greek scholar, Mr. Butcher, that "intellectual training is an end in itself, and not a mere preparation for a trade or a profession;" until we begin to understand that there is a leisure which does not mean an easy sauntering through life, but a special form of activity, employing all our faculties, and training us to the adequate reception of whatever is most valuable in literature and art; until we learn to estimate the fruits of self-culture at their proper worth, we are still far from reaping the harvest of three centuries of toil and struggle; we are still as remote as ever from the serenity of intellectual accomplishment.

There is a strange pleasure in work wedded to leisure, in work which has grown beautiful because its rude necessities are softened and humanized by sentiment and the subtle grace of association. A little paragraph from the journal of Eugenie de Guerin illustrates with charming simplicity the gilding of common toil by the delicate touch of a cultivated and sympathetic intelligence:

> A day spent in spreading out a large wash leaves little to say, and yet it is rather pretty, too, to lay the white linen on the grass, or to see it float on lines. One may fancy one's self Homer's Nausicaa, or one of those Biblical princesses who washed their brother's tunics. We have a basin at Moulinasse that you have never seen, sufficiently large, and full to the brim of water. It embellishes the hollow, and attracts the birds who like a cool place to sing in.

In the same spirit, Maurice de Guerin confesses frankly the pleasure he takes in gathering fagots for the winter fire, "that little task of the woodcutter which brings us close to nature," and which was

■ ■ ■   Crafting the Personal Essay

also a favorite occupation of M. de Lamennais. The fagot gathering, indeed, can hardly be said to have assumed the proportions of real toil; it was rather a pastime where play was thinly disguised by a pretty semblance of drudgery. "Idleness," admits de Guerin, "but idleness full of thought, and alive to every impression." Eugenie's labors, however, had other aspects and bore different fruit. There is nothing intrinsically charming in stitching seams, hanging out clothes, or scorching one's fingers over a kitchen fire; yet every page in the journal of this nobly born French girl reveals to us the nearness of work, work made sacred by the prompt fulfillment of visible duties, and what is more rare made beautiful by that distinction of mind which was the result of alternating hours of finely cultivated leisure. A very ordinary and estimable young woman might have spread her wash upon the grass with honest pride at the whiteness of her linen; but it needed the solitude of Le Cayla, the few books, well read and well worth reading, the life of patriarchal simplicity, and the habit of sustained and delicate thought, to awaken in the worker's mind the graceful association of ideas, the pretty picture of Nausicaa and her maidens cleansing their finely woven webs in the cool, rippling tide.

For it is self-culture that warms the chilly earth wherein no good seed can mature; it is self-culture that distinguishes between the work which has inherent and lasting value and the work which represents conscientious activity and no more. And for the training of one's self, leisure is requisite; leisure and that rare modesty which turns a man's thoughts back to his own shortcomings and requirements, and extinguishes in him the burning desire to enlighten his fellow-beings. "We might make ourselves spiritual by detaching ourselves from action, and become perfect by the rejection of energy," says Mr. Oscar Wilde, who delights in scandalizing his patient readers, and who lapses unconsciously into something resembling animation over the wrongs inflicted by the solemn preceptors of mankind. The notion that it is worthwhile to learn a thing only if you intend to impart it to others is widespread and exceedingly popular. I have myself heard an excellent and anxious aunt say to her young niece, then working hard at college, "But, my dear, why do you give so much of your time to Greek? You don't expect to teach it, do you?" as if there were no other use to be gained, no other pleasure to be won from that noble language, in which lies hidden the hoarded treasure of centuries. To study Greek in order to read and enjoy it, and thereby make life better worth the living, is a possibility that seldom enters the practical modern mind.

REPPLIER HAS TURNED her essay back to a discussion of the individual and what is sometimes called "learning for learning's sake." It sounds dated, certainly, to hear her talk of "noble impulses" and "the burning desire to enlighten," but underneath the verbal flourishes, she is essentially pondering issues that remain contentious even today. We find echoes of Repplier's arguments in disputes over what should be taught in our schools and universities, in debates over public funding of the arts, and in discussions of whether too much "trash" television is detrimental to the individual and to the society.

Of course, back in 1893, television was not the culprit, but people such as Repplier were still concerned that society was dumbing down.

Repplier is nearing the finish line of her contemplative essay. You will see below that she attempts to bolster her argument further by invoking Charles Lamb and Sir Walter Scott. To my contemporary ear, she has gone considerably overboard with the continuous citations of what other serious thinkers and authors have said, but she is in fact only following the norms of essay writing in her time.

Crafting the Personal Essay

Perhaps, though, she does sense the weightiness of her essay's accumulated examples, which may be why she is careful to invoke a humorous story near the end, one in which Dr. Johnson points to his travelling companion Boswell and announces: "He was idle in Edinburgh. His father sent him to Glasgow, where he continued to be idle. He came to London, where he has been very idle. And now he is going to Utrecht, where he will be as idle as ever."

Yet this restless desire to give out information, like alms, is at best a questionable bounty; this determination to share one's wisdom with one's unwilling fellow-creatures is a noble impulse provocative of general discontent. When Southey, writing to James Murray about a dialogue which he proposes to publish in the "Quarterly," says, with characteristic complacency: "I have very little doubt that it will excite considerable attention, and lead many persons into a wholesome train of thought," we feel at once how absolutely familiar is the sentiment, and how absolutely hopeless is literature approached in this spirit. The same principle, working under different conditions today, entangles us in a network of lectures, which have become the chosen field for every educational novelty, and the diversion of the mentally unemployed.

Charles Lamb has recorded distinctly his veneration for the old-fashioned schoolmaster who taught his Greek and Latin in leisurely fashion day after day, with no thought wasted upon more superficial or practical acquirements, and who "came to his task as to a sport." He has made equally plain his aversion for the new fangled pedagogue new in his time, at least who could not "relish a beggar or a gypsy" without seeking to collect or to impart some statistical information on the subject. A gentleman of this caliber, his fellow-traveler in a coach, once asked him if he had ever made "any calculation as to the value of the rental of all the retail shops in London?" and the magnitude of the question so overwhelmed Lamb that he could not even stammer out a confession of his ignorance. "To go preach to the first passer-by, to become tutor to the ignorance of the first thing I meet, is a task I abhor," observes Montaigne, who must certainly have been the most acceptable companion of his day.

Dr. Johnson, too, had scant sympathy with insistent and arrogant industry. He could work hard enough when circumstances demanded it; but he "always felt an inclination to do nothing," and not infrequently gratified his desires. "No man, sir, is obliged to do as much as he can. A man should have part of his life to himself," was the good doctor's soundly heterodox view, advanced upon many occasions. He hated to hear people boast of their assiduity, and nipped such vain pretensions in the bud with frosty scorn. When he and Boswell journeyed together in the Harwich stage-coach, "a fat, elderly gentle-woman," who had been talking freely of her own affairs, wound up by saying that she never permitted any of her children to be for a moment idle. "I wish, madam," said Dr. Johnson testily," that you would educate me too, for I have been an idle fellow all my life." "I am sure, sir," protested the woman with dismayed politeness, "you have not been idle." "Madam," was the retort, "it is true! And that gentleman there," pointing to poor young Boswell, "has been idle also. He was idle in Edinburgh. His father sent him to Glasgow, where he continued to be idle. He came to London, where he has been very idle. And now he is going to Utrecht, where he will be as idle as ever."

That there was a background of truth in these spirited assertions we have every reason to be grateful. Dr. Johnson's value today does not depend on the number of essays, reviews, or dedications he wrote in a year, —some years he wrote nothing, —but on his own sturdy and splendid personality; "the real primate, the soul's teacher of all England," says Carlyle; a great embodiment of uncompromising goodness and sense. Every generation needs such a man, not to compile dictionaries, but to preserve the balance of sanity, and few generations are blest enough to possess him. As for Boswell, he might have toiled in the law courts until he was gray without benefiting or amusing anybody. It was in the nights he spent drinking port wine at the Mitre, and in the days he spent trotting, like a terrier, at his master's heels, that the seed was sown which was to give the world a masterpiece of literature, the most delightful biography that has ever enriched mankind. It is to leisure that we owe the "Life of Johnson," and a heavy debt we must, in all integrity, acknowledge it to be.

Mr. Shortreed said truly of Sir Walter Scott that he was "making himself in the busy, idle pleasures of his youth;" in those long rambles by hill and dale, those whimsical adventures in farmhouses, those merry, purposeless journeys in which the eager lad tasted the flavor of life. At home such unauthorized amusements were regarded with emphatic disapprobation. "I greatly doubt, sir," said his father to him one day, "that you were born for nae better than a gangrel scrape-gut!" and one half pities the grave clerk to the Signet, whose own life had been so decorously dull, and who regarded with affectionate solicitude his lovable and incomprehensible son. In later years Sir Walter recognized keenly that his wasted school hours entailed on him a lasting loss, a loss he was determined his sons should never know. It is to be forever regretted that "the most Homeric of modern men could not read Homer." But every day he stole from the town to give to the country, every hour he stole from law to give to literature, every minute he stole from work to give to pleasure, counted in the end as gain. It is in his pleasures that a man really lives, it is from his leisure that he constructs the true fabric of self. Perhaps Charles Lamb's fellow- clerks thought that because his days were spent at a desk in the East India House, his life was spent there too. His life was far remote from that routine of labor; built up of golden moments of respite, enriched with joys, chastened by sorrows, vivified by impulses that had no filiation with his daily toil. "For the time that a man may call his own," he writes to Wordsworth, "that is his life." The Lamb who worked in the India House, and who had "no skill in figures," has passed away, and is today but a shadow and a name. The Lamb of the "Essays" and the "Letters" lives for us now, and adds each year his generous share to the innocent gayety of the world. This is the Lamb who said, "Riches are chiefly good because they give us time," and who sighed for a little son that he might christen him Nothing-to-do, and permit him to do nothing.

AND THUS, SHE ends her contemplation and *assaying*, having suggested not only that leisure is good for the soul and for society as a whole, but also that some of the most valuable contributions to a society (from the likes of Sir Walter Scott and Charles Lamb) derive from an individual's leisurely pursuit, rather than from hard labor, or what is sometimes called "the American work ethic."

It may have occurred to you by now that Repplier is essentially arguing for her own right to do what she does: The contemplative essayist, after all, is one who takes time to stare at the clouds, and one who reads and writes for the sake of knowledge and enlightenment rather than for mere commercial gain.

I would not advise you to follow Repplier's prose style if you plan to reach a twenty-first-century audience of readers, but I certainly think even now we can follow her sage advice. Weighing one's thoughts, writing them down, revising for clarity, all take time, and there is no way that the process can be hurried.

PURSUING MENTAL RABBITS

"The pursuit of truth and beauty is a sphere of activity in which we are permitted to remain children all our lives."
—Albert Einstein

When I was roughly ten-years old, my cousins kept a beagle named Smokey, and, let me tell you, that dog truly loved to wander. Sometimes he would meander down to the bay and roll in the foul-smelling corpses of beached catfish and carp. I can't explain why this seemed so pleasurable to the dog, but he absolutely loved it, and I recall as if yesterday those times my Aunt Grace would open the side screen door to let the dog back in at the end of the day and end up shouting, "Oh, no! Out in the yard with you, stinker."

Then she'd get the hose.

What Smokey loved even more than the stench of rotting fish, however, was to chase rabbits. He was a speedy dog, and my cousin Desi and I would often catch a glimpse of the beagle flashing across one of the neighbor's broad lawns, in hot pursuit. On occasion, that would be our last glimpse of Smokey for one or two days. He would disappear like that but always came back.

As a youngster, I imagined that Smokey was chasing that same unfortunate rabbit all the way across town, through the night, into the next morning, but now that I'm older and can take a moment to examine my memory, it seems obvious enough that he probably only chased the rabbit through two or three backyards, lost track, ran across an intriguing smell in the grass, tracked the source of that aroma for a while, lost the scent, and then saw something else—another rabbit, a paperboy on a bike, a female poodle—and started yet another chase.

For Smokey, the world was an endless source of fast-moving objects and interesting smells.

Pulitzer Prize nominee Scott Russell Sanders must have known a dog like Smokey, because he has compared the art of essay writing to "the pursuit of mental rabbits," invoking the idea that a successful essay is a hunt, a chase, a ramble through thickets of thought, in pursuit of some brief glimmer of fuzzy truth. He knew that the spirit of Smokey the beagle can be found in the best personal essayists (minus, we hope, the rolling in the fish).

 WRITING EXERCISE: "I'M GONNA GET THAT RASCALLY RABBIT!"

Pick one childhood memory: something seemingly inconsequential but fun to remember, like my Smokey the beagle story. Maybe for you it is a hole in the back fence that opened into a field, a broad limb of a tree that made for comfortable sitting, the coolness of your grandmother's basement in the summer, or the day your mother put Kool-Aid in the ice tray and surprised you and your friends with homemade popsicles.

Crafting the Personal Essay

Capture that memory as best you can on the page, but then go on a chase, ramble through thickets of thought, pursue your own brief glimmer of fuzzy truth. Why do you retain the memory of that moment all of these years later? Other than just being a pleasant recollection, what deeper resonance is hidden in your story? What have you lost over the years, and can you ever get it back?

THE MOVEMENT OF THE ESSAY

There is a wonderful freedom in the essay, a rare permission to follow one's curiosity wherever it may lead. But with this freedom comes the challenge of how to insure coherent movement and interest for the reader.

Or to put it another way, there is the gentle ramble through lovely forest on a leaf-strewn path, and then there is getting lost, getting annoyed, and wondering what the heck you walked into the woods for in the first place. Which experience do you suppose the reader enjoys best?

Writers of memoir (like fiction writers) most often rely on the arc of a story to structure a piece of prose. This normal story arc usually includes a scene or scenes that explain what happened on a particular day or week, who was there, what was said or done, and the consequences of that action. The question in a reader's mind that keeps the pages turning is usually "so what happened next?"

Even if chronology is rearranged, through the use of flashbacks, flash forwards, and other narrative devices, the basic "what happened from moment to moment" is there to keep order and suggest structure.

Because the personal essay is often less "story driven," however, we need to view structure in new ways.

"No one is freer than the essayist—free to leap out in any direction, to hop from thought to thought, to begin with the finish and finish with the middle, or to eschew beginning and end and keep only a middle," essayist Cynthia Ozick reminds us. "The marvel is that out of this apparent cause-lessness, out of this scattering of idiosyncratic seeing and telling, a coherent world is made."

Sounds good, but how is that coherent world made, when we know full well our thoughts and mental pursuits are often haphazard at best? Doesn't a rabbit merely zig and zag in no logical direction, and if we are chasing that rabbit, aren't we just zigging and zagging wildly as well?

Well, the simple answer, remember, is that the unstructured feel of the essay is an illusion. Successful writers revise and revise and revise until the words and the sentences and the paragraphs and the order in which the paragraphs appear seem to fall naturally into place. It is a wonderful illusion, not dissimilar to watching a juggler effortlessly circling nine balls in the air. The truth is that the juggler practiced for years and dropped nine thousand balls in order to master this "effortless" presentation. Similarly, the writer whose work seems graceful and natural is probably the writer who has worked hardest on arranging and rearranging and rearranging again.

But where is this order to be found if there is no natural narrative arc in the mental pursuit of an essay? Where is the connective tissue?

Let's look at how various contemporary essayists have tackled this challenge.

Begin Small

As Virginia Woolf demonstrated with her essay on the moth, even the least of things can hold the key to a universe of meaning.

Author Lia Purpura, in her essay "Glaciology," teaches a similar lesson, beginning with this description of the debris littered beneath a bank of snow:

> When the snow began to melt, the drifts left be-
> hind a surprising collection of junk—paper cups,
> socks, Matchbox trucks, a snarl of CAUTION–
> POLICE–CAUTION tape, pinkly wrapped tampons,
> oil-rag-T-shirts, banana peels: intimacies of toy
> box, bathroom, and garage amid the lumps of
> sand and salt we threw down for traction. It was
> as if after the big event of snowfall we'd forgotten
> there was more, still, to be said.

Purpura uses this image of scattered junk to move from a consideration of urban detritus to thoughts on deposits of another kind, announcing in the next paragraph, "I shall make my own study of snow and time. I will learn from that which has built the very ground I'm now slipping around on: glaciers."

And true to her word, she quickly and deftly (the attentive reader does not get lost along the way) transitions from the trash on the sidewalk to the rock debris and sediment left behind by glacial movement and how these deposits can help geologists trace the path of the ice.

This, then, starts Purpura to thinking: Aren't the artifacts of a human life—both the physical objects we accumulate and the experiences we have—something like that rock debris and sediment, and don't these artifacts help us to track the movement of a human life?

The answer, of course, is yes, and soon enough Purpura is tracking small moments in her own life, and this essay on the rubble beneath a snow bank becomes deeply personal:

> Waiting all that long week—for test results, the snow
> to stop, dough to rise, nightfall—small tasks turned
> into days. ... And though dressing for sledding, un-
> dressing and draping everything wet over radiators
> was deliberate, a stitch ran through, jagged and
> taut, cinching the gestures tight with uncertainty.

The author is awaiting medical test results, and her essay moves swiftly from the initial "paper cups, socks, Matchbox trucks" under the snow to the rocks and sediment left behind by the scraping of glacial ice to these small tasks of folding her family's laundry, making popcorn, drying clothes after a morning of sledding, little rocks left behind in the path of her life.

She promised us early in the essay that she would make her "own study of snow and time" and she has done just that. The connective tissue of her narrative is the repeated imagery of deposits, sediments, small artifacts remaining behind to tell the larger story. The "journey" or narrative arc of her essay is the movement of her thoughts during this week that every little task seemed to take on a greater significance, a week where "joy and severity flared everywhere."

It has been said that poetry is that which cannot be para-phrased, and it is similarly hard to do a complex, meandering lyric essay such as Purpura's justice in simple summary, but the essay ends with good news—"I was negative. *Negative, negative*, I was thinking, buoyant. The hard winter lifted all at once, the sun came, dewy and beading, the air was sweet and I was fine"—and the journey is complete.

Remember, You Are Not a Cat

For my cousin's beagle, the world was an endless source of fast-moving objects and interesting smells. This is true as well for most writers, and certainly for those who pursue the personal essay. Curiosity may have killed the cat, but not you.

And not Scott Russell Sanders, the essayist to whom I am indebted for the "pursuit of mental rabbits" metaphor. Sanders' essay "Beauty" begins in church, the morning of his daughter's wedding:

> In memory, I wait beside Eva in the vestibule of the church to play my bit part as father of the bride. She hooks a hand on my elbow while three brides- maids fuss over her, fixing the gauzy veil, spread- ing the long ivory train of her gown, tucking into her bun a loose strand of hair, which glows the color of honey filled with sunlight. Clumsy in my rented patent leather shoes and stiff black tux- edo, I stand among these gorgeous women like a crow among doves. I realize they're gorgeous not because they carry bouquets or wear silk dresses, but because the festival of marriage has slowed time down until any fool can see their glory.

The happy occasion he writes about with such loving details becomes an occasion for Sanders to meditate on the work- ing of memory, and on how, two months after the wedding is over, he "can summon up hundreds of details from that radiant day," though on the day he felt unaware of all that was happening around him, distracted by his own "sur- passing joy."

Perhaps, he writes, the "glow of happiness had to cool before it would crystallize into memory."

And then:

> Pardon my cosmic metaphor, but I can't help think- ing of the physicists' claim that, if we trace the

universe back to its origins in the Big Bang, we find
the multiplicity of things fusing into greater and
greater simplicity, until at the moment of creation
itself there is only pure undifferentiated energy.
Without being able to check their equations, I think
the physicists are right. I believe the energy they
speak of is holy, by which I mean it is the closest
we can come with our instruments to measuring
the strength of God.

Sanders certainly doesn't shy away from weighty subjects—
the Big Bang, the moment of creation, the existence of God.
If I thought this essay was in less-skilled hands, I'd be tempted to say the author has bitten off more than can be chewed
and digested, but Sanders is a master of the form.

But You Can Be the Great Celestial Puppeteer ...

Sanders goes on to invoke the Milky Way, the Hubble Tele-
scope, and the Cat's Eye Nebula, but he never goes all wob-
bly on us, never allows his essay to spin out of control like
some science fiction space capsule that has suddenly fallen
out of orbit.

Sanders remembers the reader, sitting there with a book
or magazine in her hand, struggling to make sense of this
wide-ranging mental expedition, and he quickly makes a
connection for us, showing his twin subjects converging in
a practical way—two sets of photos in his study:

On these cool September mornings, I've been
poring over two sets of photographs, those from
deep space and those from Eva's wedding, trying to figure out why such different images—of

supernova and shining daughter, of spinning
galaxies and trembling bouquets—set up in me
the same hum of delight. The feeling is unusually
intense for me just now, so soon after the nuptials, but it has never been rare. As far back as I
can remember, things seen or heard or smelled,
things tasted or touched, have provoked in me
an answering vibration.

Read that previous paragraph at least twice. There is plenty
going on in just those few simple sentences: an image of the
author looking at two sets of photos explaining why he is
simultaneously thinking about the wedding and about the
physics of space, the interweaving of imagery such as "supernova and shining daughter ... spinning galaxies and
trembling bouquets," and the muted admission that such
intense reverie is unusual, but maybe can be excused since
it is "so soon after the nuptials." Finally, there is an explanation: The author has always felt certain sensations with
great intensity.

Sanders, consciously or instinctively, is aware that the
reader may be close to becoming overwhelmed, so he is
taking a breath, slowing down intentionally, allowing the
reader to relax before the essay moves on. More importantly,
Sanders is reassuring us that he is firmly in control of his
far-reaching deliberation.

Sanders is not the only one prone to cosmic imagery.
One of my favorite metaphors when teaching the personal
essay is the idea of an invisible gravitational pull. "Ideas
might begin to float off," I tell my students, "but they can't
go too far, because they are locked into the gravity of the
home planet. Every idea is a small moon, each of these small

moons has certain freedom of movement, but the planet always rules."

The home planet in this metaphor is the true subject of the essay and as a writer you are, for once in your life, the great celestial puppeteer, deciding which planet will rule and how the gravity will play itself out.

Enjoy.

... Or Become the Earthly Architect

Though the sense that one is following the free-form meandering of an author's curious mind (chasing those mental rabbits) is the most common method of creating structure and forward movement in an essay, it is by no means the only available option.

On certain occasions, an author might decide to invent a deliberate structure to give order to his personal essays.

While most of my nonfiction writing follows a pretty traditional path, I have also composed essays that mimic the form of a coroner's report, a made-for-television movie script, and a Zen koan. One of my favorite experiments, "Son of Mr. Green Jeans: An Essay on Fatherhood, Alphabetically Arranged," borrows a form knows as abecedarium from the world of poetry.

An abecedarium can look like this popular song from the 1920s:

A – You're Adorable
B – You're so Beautiful
C – You're a Cutie full of Charm ...

Or it can be something more complex. In fact, the abecedarium traces back at least as far as the eighth century, with the Anglo-Saxon Rune Poem, the Norwegian Rune Poem, and the Icelandic Rune Poem. But it always follows the letters of the alphabet, in order.

For *my* "Son of Mr. Green Jeans" essay, since I was writing prose not poetry, instead of having each line begin with a letter of the alphabet, I allowed myself encyclopedia-like entries while still limiting myself to *a* through *z*, in alphabetical order.

Let me show you the first three entries in my oddly structured exploration of fatherhood and popular culture:

Allen, Tim

Best known as the father on ABC's *Home Improvement* (1991–99), the popular comedian was born Timothy Allen Dick on June 13, 1953. When Allen was eleven-years old, his father, Gerald Dick, was killed by a drunk driver while driving home from a University of Colorado football game.

Bees

"A man, after impregnating the woman, could drop dead," critic Camille Paglia suggested to Tim Allen in a 1995 *Esquire* interview. "That is how peripheral he is to the whole thing."

"I'm a drone," Allen responded. "Like those bees."

"You are a drone," Paglia agreed. "That's exactly right."

Carp

After the female Japanese Carp gives birth to hundreds of tiny babies, the father carp remains nearby. When he senses approaching danger, he

> sucks the helpless babies into his mouth, and
> holds them there until the coast is clear.

This form allows me to introduce in quick succession three recurring threads that will form the fabric of my essay—absent fathers, the role that men play in the development of children, and how fathering occurs in the animal world. (Or in this case, the fish world.)

I won't take you through every letter of the alphabet, but I next introduce Divorce, Emperor Penguins, my memories of the 1960s TV show *Father Knows Best*, and some information on Irish genetic history, under the heading (and playful pun on the title) "Green Genes."

Then I move on to another TV show that was important to me as a child, before using the heading Inheritance to move the essay into more personal territory.

Hugh Beaumont

The actor who portrayed the benevolent father on the popular TV show *Leave it to Beaver* was a Methodist minister. Tony Dow, who played older brother Wally, reports that Beaumont actually hated kids. "Hugh wanted out of the show after the second season," Dow told the *Toronto Sun*. "He thought he should be doing films and things."

Inheritance

My own Irish forefather was a newspaperman, owned a nightclub, ran for mayor, and smuggled rum in a speedboat during Prohibition. He smoked, drank, ate nothing but red meat, and died of a heart attack in 1938.

Crafting the Personal Essay

His one son, my father, was a teenager when my grandfather died. I never learned more than the barest details about my grandfather from my father, despite my persistent questions. Other relatives tell me that the relationship had been strained.

My father was a skinny, asthmatic, and eager to please little boy, not the tough guy his father had wanted. He lost his mother at age three, and later developed a severe stuttering problem, perhaps as a result of his father's disapproval. My father's adult vocabulary was outstanding, due to his need for alternate words when faltering over hard consonants like B or D.

The stuttering grew worse over the years, with one exception: After downing a few whiskeys, my father could sing like an angel. His Irish tenor became legend in local taverns, and by the time I entered the scene my father was spending every evening visiting the bars. Most nights he would stumble back drunk around midnight; some nights he was so drunk he would stumble through a neighbor's back door, thinking he was home.

As a boy, I coped with the family's embarrassment by staying glued to the television—shows like *Father Knows Best* and *Leave it to Beaver* were my favorites. I desperately wanted someone like Hugh Beaumont to be my father, or maybe Robert Young.

Hugh Brannum, though, would have been my first choice. Brannum played Mr. Green Jeans on *Captain Kangaroo*, and I remember him as being kind, funny, and extremely reliable.

Now all of the varied threads are in play, and I have room to explore some other examples from the animal kingdom and additional aspects of 1960s television families.

Eventually, I bring the reader to the central subject of my essay—my reluctance at age thirty to become a father myself, primarily because of the disparities between these "squeaky clean and always jovial" fathers on television and my own experience growing up in a troubled household.

Take a look at the entry for *N*:

Natural Selection

When my wife Renita confessed to me her ambition to have children, the very first words out of my mouth were, "You must be crazy." Convinced that she had just proposed the worst imaginable idea, I stood from my chair, looked straight ahead, and then marched out of the room.

That's a true story, and certainly not my best moment as a husband.

Q was difficult, but since this essay is at its heart highly playful, I was able to throw in a Quiz:

Quiz

1. What is Camille Paglia's view on the need for fathers?
2. Why did Hugh Beaumont hate kids?
3. Who played Mr. Green Jeans on *Captain Kangaroo*?
4. Who would you rather have as your father: Hugh Beaumont, Hugh Brannum, a wolf, or an emperor penguin?

I move forward in the alphabet, jumping between popular culture, zoology, and my own story, until I come to *W*, which through an act of writing serendipity, allowed me to find the perfect entry for the potentially troublesome *X*.

Ward's Father

In an episode titled "Beaver's Freckles," the Beaver says that Ward had "a hittin' father," but little else is ever revealed about Ward's fictional family. Despite Wally's constant warning—"Boy, Beav, when Dad finds out, he's gonna clobber ya!"—Ward does not follow his own father's example, and never hits his sons on the show. This is an excellent example of xenogenesis.

Xenogenesis

(zen"u-jen'u-sis), n. Biol. 1. heterogenesis 2. the supposed generation of offspring completely and permanently different from the parent.

Believing in xenogenesis—though at the time I couldn't define it, spell it, *or* pronounce it—I changed my mind about having children about four years after my wife's first suggestion of the idea.

Since I am in fact the author of this essay, I don't really need to speculate as to what might have been going through the writer's mind.

I know.

The truth is, I had been working off-and-on for three years on this short piece, and for almost all of that time the essay-in-progress was a pretty conventional look at differing views of human fathering and fatherhood in the mammal world.

It was also painfully dull.

I would work on it for a week, get stuck and discouraged, and stuff it in a drawer. Some months later, after distracting myself with some other writing project, I would pull it out again, work some, get stuck, yawn, and stuff it away once more.

Only after repeated attempts to "fix" what was not working in the essay did I hit on the experimental form. "Hmmm," I thought to myself, "I have lots of animal examples—carp, penguin, wolf, guppy, chimpanzee—maybe I should put them in alphabetical order." Once I did that, it occurred to me to flesh out the entire alphabet by adding in popular culture references, especially the "perfect fathers" of those idealized television comedies.

Before long, the essay was becoming five times more interesting.

MY ASSAY: WHEREIN THE AUTHOR ATTEMPTS TO FOLLOW HIS OWN ADVICE

I've made a discovery while working on the early drafts of my essay "On Foot." What I've realized is that I need to pursue my own mental rabbits and determine why it bothered me so much that no one but me seemed to be out walking the sidewalks of Boca Raton the week that I visited. Why do I value the art of sauntering so much? Where is my discomfort, or indignation, coming from?

Well, I think it has to do with my own childhood. Further, it might be the manner in which that childhood formed my sense of how a community is formed.

All I have right now is a general concept—my childhood—and an abstract idea—how communities form and stay healthy. I have yet to need to find the words that will make these abstract notions tangible and resonant on the page, but I'm fairly sure that's where the essay is headed.

Of course, now I have three of four threads to worry about, but for the moment I'm not too concerned with fitting them together. I like to use the analogy of building a clay brick wall. (Imagine for a moment that you have to hand-form these bricks from the clay you've dug out of the soil, and then bake them yourself, since there is no Home Depot in this metaphor.) Well, first you make the bricks, and then you stack them off to the side. My tentative opening is a brick, my story about Boca is another few bricks, and my ideas about childhood and community will be baked into bricks as well.

I'm stacking these bricks into rough piles for the moment, because I'm not really sure what my wall will look like in the end.

WHY WE CHASE THE RABBITS

A beagle chases a rabbit for two reasons, I think (though admittedly, I've never been able to get a beagle to tell me for himself):

1) He honestly believes that if he ever catches that elusive rabbit, it will somehow be well worth the effort, and

2) Chasing rabbits is fun.

Writing is no different—the effort pays off eventually, but along with the hard work, always remember to keep the spirit of playful exploration alive.

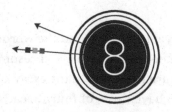

WRITING THE LYRIC ESSAY

"Like a poem, a genuine essay is made of language and character and mood and temperament and pluck and chance."
—Cynthia Ozick

If you think back to why you first fell in love with writing—and I mean, *way* back—it probably wasn't because of plot, structure, theme, description, and dialogue, or any of the other fine points of literary craft. It was most likely just words. Language.

Just as very small children find the act of stringing two or three words together to form a sentence—"Daddy funny hat!"—enormously exhilarating, some of us felt this same curious thrill when putting our first words down on paper.

Maybe it was a poem:

> My kitten
> yellow fuzzy
> everywhere

Or maybe it was just individual words, made permanent by our own hands.

Those words represented ideas, emotions, things, and even in second grade, well before we could compose our first coherent paragraph, we sensed the power and possibilities.

That's where writers begin, I believe, and that initial impulse needn't be abandoned just because we have grown into our intellect, logic, and sense of order.

The essay used as an example in the previous chapter, Lia Purpura's "Glaciology," retains some of that love for language play. For instance, look at Purpura's description of the way in which snow melts where it has been piled up in a parking lot, forming a shape almost spinelike, with individual vertebrae:

> Bones stacked and bent in the attitude of prayer,
> the edges honed and precarious ... The shapes
> were knife-edged, hunched, easing a pain; they
> grayed and were everywhere pocked with dirt,
> and unlikely in their strength.

That passage relies as much on the author's choice of words—"bones ... honed ... knife-edged, hunched ... pocked with dirt"—for energy as it does on any underlying idea or logical connection. Purpura is letting the sheer musicality and evocativeness of language create part of the experience for her readers.

Of course, there is nothing really new about this; poets, playwrights, short story writers, and novelists have always used these tools to evoke an emotional reaction in the reader. But often, it seemed, nonfiction writers were being asked to keep the "fancy" language out of the work. Perhaps because of our proximity to journalism, and ultimately to what is sometimes called "the factual record," writers of nonfiction felt constrained and limited.

Two editors working with a small literary journal, Deborah Tall and John D'Agata, have helped to champion a movement that encourages essayists to push the boundaries wherever they might lead. In a 1997 issue of the *Seneca Review*, Tall and D'Agata offered this open-ended description for what they termed the "lyric essay:"

> The lyric essay partakes of the poem in its density and shapeliness, its distillation of ideas and musicality of language. It partakes of the essay in its weight, in its overt desire to engage with facts, melding its allegiance to the actual with its passion for imaginative form ... The lyric essay ... elucidates through the dance of its own delving.

The work that has resulted, in *Seneca Review* and other venues, has certainly lived up to the challenge.

A Note on Self-Indulgence

Having fun with language, making imaginative leaps and idiosyncratic jumps, "beaming" from idea to idea like Captain Kirk of the Starship Enterprise transporting between planets, is a great place to start. This is where surprise and discovery most often occur—in the realm of the experimental and unexpected. After all, if writers followed only predictable paths, where would new ideas come from?

But having such fun for yourself is only the beginning. The reader must somehow follow the movement of your thoughts, language, and intuition, and must feel some unspoken harmony behind your words and images, or you are writing for an audience of one. Unless you plan to buy thousands of copies of your own first book, that's not such a good idea.

Luckily, the reader is very agile and mostly willing.

"Essay writing is about transcribing the often convoluted process of thought," suggests essayist Lauren Slater, "leaving your own brand of bread crumbs in the forest so that those who want to can find their way to your door."

So go ahead and have fun with words and lyric dances of your own delving.

Just remember that eventually—and this might not be until you are five or fifteen drafts into the writing—you must find a way to leave your own "bread crumbs in the forest," so that the reader can follow along.

Three Quick Tips

• Densely poetic writing demands careful attention. Listen to the encouraging words of Annie Dillard: "When I gave up writing poetry I was very sad, for I had devoted fifteen years to the study of how the structures of poems carry meaning. But I was delighted to find that nonfiction prose can also carry meaning in its structures and, like poetry, can tolerate all sorts of figurative language, as well as alliteration and even rhyme. The range of rhythms in prose is larger and grander than it is in poetry, and it can handle discursive ideas and plain information as well as character and story. It can do everything. I felt as though I had switched from a single reed instrument to a full orchestra." That's a pretty strong endorsement for the use of figurative language and other poetic devices in your writing, but heed Dillard's final metaphor. It is better, perhaps, to control an entire orchestra rather than just one flute, but it takes infinitely more work and practice.

• Read other lyric essays for inspiration. In addition to Lia Purpura, look for work by contemporary essayists Eula Biss, Brenda Miller, Donald Morrill, and Mary Ruefle, or look at some of the more experimental prose from classic writers such as Virginia Woolf.

- Expect resistance. Don't be surprised if some in your writing group question what you are doing. Listen to their advice, but if they are pushing you to write safely, to sound like everyone else, you can politely ignore their advice after giving it fair consideration.

YOUR LYRIC ESSAY

As always, these prompts are suggestions. They are not carved in stone and needn't be followed too strictly.

Just see where they lead, and always hold on to you spirit of playfulness.

1. Try to sound like Lia Purpura. You won't, of course, not in the end, because style is personal. Mimicry, however, can be a valuable first step to expanding one's range (in guitar work, in painting, in writing.) So take a portion of an essay you are still working on, or start something new, and for a draft or two, attempt to follow Purpura's unique rhythms and wordplay. Maybe you'll decide that isn't your style and change it all back. Or maybe you'll discover something new in your own style.

2. List and catalog. Remember the first paragraph from "Glaciology," where Purpura itemized the diverse objects revealed under the melting snow? Open a drawer, in your kitchen or in your memory, and just list what is found, but try to make the language and description sing with poetry of its own.

3. Jenny Boully, another contemporary writer who has embraced the lyric essay idea, once wrote an entire essay that was nothing but blank pages, recalling

Crafting the Personal Essay

those 1960s painters who hung pure white canvasses in galleries to make a point about art. Boully, however, offered more than just conceptual trickery: Her blank essay had eighty footnotes, and she put these extended footnotes at the bottom of every blank page. By following the footnotes, an odd and fascinating story begins to form in the blank space she left on top. What would happen if you wrote an essay that was nothing but footnotes, or nothing but comments on an empty blog entry, or just a series of Facebook status updates?

4. Essayist and novelist David Shields has written, "Genre is a minimum-security prison." Once we say "this is an essay" or "this is a poem," we begin to think there are rules to be followed. What if you just wrote and didn't worry until draft twenty what it was you were actually writing?

5. Write an essay in five paragraphs. Each sentence in the first paragraph must begin with *E*. Each sentence in the second paragraph must begin with *S*. For the third, *S* again. For the fourth, each sentence must begin with the letter *A*. And finally, for the final paragraph, start each sentence with the letter *Y*. (Get it? E_S_S_A_Y.)

6. My essay discussed in the previous chapter, "Son of Mr. Green Jeans," came about because the alphabet form forced me to go in directions I would not have gone otherwise. Take an essay you are working on but have not completed, maybe one that has been frustrating you for some time, and freewrite

for fifteen minutes on alternate structures. Write down every goofy idea you have.

7. Write an essay of twelve short paragraphs. Then roll a pair of dice to see which paragraph comes first, which comes second, and so on. Cut and paste into the new order. What is the result?

8. Words are beautiful in and of themselves. The shriek of gulls. The scuttling of a crab. The imbrication of wave onto shore. Attempt an essay that is nothing but phrases or incomplete sentences that exist only because the words themselves are powerful.

9. Write an essay entitled "Turquoise," that is about many things, all tied together by color. Or maybe "Burnt Umber."

10. Can a crossword puzzle be an essay? Is there a true story being told in the clues?

OF CONFLICT

"The test of a first-rate intelligence is the ability to hold two opposing ideas in mind at the same time and still retain the ability to function."
—F. Scott Fitzgerald

Over the years, in the many college writing workshops I've been privileged to teach, countless students have written essays reflecting on the death of a grandparent. Until recently, every one of these essays centered on how much the writer missed this grandparent, and how hard it was to believe that Gramma or Pop-Pop was actually gone.

The better of these essays devoted a paragraph or two to bringing the deceased relative back to life—"Grandma Sophia would cook for the entire family every Sunday, and I can still see the tiny smile she wore when her wrinkled hands carefully rolled the perfect meatballs one after the other and placed them in the pan"—so that the reader might feel the loss as well.

But it wasn't until this past year that a student, Kate, wrote a grandparent essay that rocked me back in my chair. Kate's grandfather had died the year before, in the same month that Kate also lost her friend Snowball, a white puff of a dog.

"I miss Snowball far more than I miss my grandfather," she wrote," because I barely miss my grandfather at all."

Now, I'm not coldhearted, nor do I want grandchildren to feel badly toward their grandparents, but this essay was suddenly far more interesting than all of the others of this variety, because it embodied one important aspect of good storytelling that the other essays seemed to lack:

Conflict.

Kate felt bad about this revelation, sensed it wasn't the way one was supposed to think or feel. She was conflicted, confused, and entirely surprised by her own reaction.

And that's a good place to begin writing.

The French word *assay*, remember, from which we came up with the word essay in the English language, means to try out, to seek an answer or solution, to attempt to make sense of something. Essayists are not pursuing mental rabbits merely for the aromatic stew of words that might ensue. The center of the essay is some question or problem that the writer is trying to solve.

Essayist and critic Phillip Lopate reminds us, "Without conflict, your essay will drift into static mode, repeating your initial observation in a self-satisfied way. What gives an essay dynamism is the need to work out some problem, especially a problem that is not easily resolved." But, the good news, he adds, is that "... human beings are conflicted animals, so there is no shortage of tensions that won't go away."

Kate worked through many drafts of her essay, and finally concluded that she misses the dog more than she misses her grandfather for a very good reason: The dog showed her more love. Her grandfather was not a bad man, not evil or abusive, but he tended to retreat into his chair at family gatherings and go silent. She loved the man well enough, perhaps out of family loyalty, felt sorry for him at times, but the truth was that he never rose to the affectionate grandfather role, and she was not going to pretend any longer.

 ## WRITING EXERCISE: I JUST DON'T UNDERSTAND YOU

Too often, we write about other people because we think we know something about that person, or because we feel that we can weigh in with intelligent correctness on their actions or the choices they have made. Too often as well, we end up sounding like mister or ms. know-it-all. Whether we are writing about a celebrity or politician, someone who lives just down the street, or a relative, like Kate's distant grandfather, the assumption that we actually know someone's motives and understand what factors into their behavior is a dicey one at best. Life is complicated, and people are hard to fathom.

So think a moment about the people you *do not* comprehend, and would never claim to fully understand, even if we thought long and hard about it. My list would include two friends who struggled to keep together a marriage but simply could not. Neither one of them was bad or at fault. They just couldn't find the working formula, and I have no better take on what they should have done instead. Still, it seems a shame.

I also can't understand a friend who repeatedly shoots herself in the foot just when her career is taking off. Clearly, she wants to succeed, just as we all do, but something deep inside is driving her to fail. Though I have observed this behavior for years, it still makes no sense to me at all.

A less serious but equally baffling example concerns the folks in my neighborhood (and in most neighborhoods, I imagine) who treat their front lawns and driveways as if they were hospital operating rooms, hosing away every leaf and acorn first thing in the morning, painstakingly digging out each dandelion and virtually every green shoot that does not look like perfect Kentucky grass. Now I like my yard to look nice, but I can't see putting eight-hours-a-week into it, and a few leaves and twigs and weeds are, to my mind, inevitable. It's autumn as I'm writing this, and not only is my lawn covered in red oak leaves, but I just noticed a stray leaf in the living room, by the front door. Mother Nature is nothing if not persistent.

Make your own list of the people who make no sense to you. You aren't firmly against their choices, and you don't have all the answers; they just baffle you. Put some real people on that list, some types of people (the lawn purists), and even some famous folks if you'd like.

Now write about what you *don't* understand, and how unsure you are about what is going on inside the mind and heart of this person. Don't attack or suggest that you know better; just explore.

PUTTING CONFLICT IN THE STORY

Charles Isherwood, theatre critic for *The New York Times*, wrote this recently:

> A primary aim of good theater is to hold the proverbial mirror up to nature, and natural man is a vexingly complicated being: a mixture of virtues and foibles, healthy impulses and irreducible neuroses,

petty desires and solid ideals. Virtually nobody in
life is a simple villain or a plain-vanilla saint ... The
best drama holds fast to the messy truth about
human motivation, and the two must-see productions to open during this chilly winter offer rich
material for ruminating on the endless surprises of
character in the crucible of circumstance.

Though Isherwood is talking about new productions of
Broadway plays, he could just as well have been speaking of
the personal essay. Ruminating on the endless surprises of
character always offers rich material, and though the inherent conflict within the human character is not the *only* place
to find energy for an essay, it remains one of the best. In fact,
look closely at Hollywood action films or books about the
Civil War or television shows based on weather and natural
disasters, and you'll see that almost all of them have one
thing in common—large external conflicts are brought to
life through human stories.

How do you bring conflict into your personal essay
and avoid what Lopate called the "static mode"? Let's look
at how various classic and contemporary essayists have
solved the problem.

Be the Provocateur

A key difference between the essay and the fictional short
story is that you, the author, are the protagonist in the essay,
the consciousness through which the world is viewed. You
are the main character, so to speak.

In fiction, of course, readers prefer a main character
with some fire in her belly, someone who sees the world
in a particular way, feels strongly about whatever problem

she is trying to solve, and takes bold actions. Think Scarlett O'Hara from the novel *Gone with the Wind*.

Readers of the essay are no different; they will tolerate some wishy-washiness in an author because they recognize that self-doubt and second-guessing are an honest part of human thought, but they still want some fire in the belly, and they still want a distinct point-of-view.

British essayist William Hazlitt, writing in the early 1800s, was a keen student of Montaigne, Joseph Addison, Samuel Johnson, and others who came before him. He also knew how to gain an audience's notice during a time when numerous British magazines and tabloids were in fierce competition for readers.

Consider the title of one of Hazlitt's better-known essays, "On the Pleasure of Hating." The conflict is right there, in those five words.

Hazlitt begins his essay remarking on a spider that had just crossed his desk. (This was before Virginia Woolf and her moth, but it does seem as if insects hold a prominent place in the classic personal essay, doesn't it?)

After introducing his wandering spider, Hazlitt writes:

> As he passes me, I lift up the matting to assist his escape, am glad to get rid of the unwelcome intruder, and shudder at the recollection after he is gone ... I bear the creature no ill-will, but still I hate the very sight of it.

And then:

> We learn to curb our will and keep our overt actions within the bounds of humanity, long before we can subdue our sentiments and imaginations to the same mild tone. We give up the external

> demonstration, the brute violence, but cannot
> part with the essence or principle of hostility.

Hazlitt has made his claim—hatred must be hidden in polite society, but it remains inside of us all the same—and though the average reader would likely be balking at this point, protesting that certainly they are not a hateful sort, Hazlitt just plunges on:

> Nature seems (the more we look into it) made
> up of antipathies: without something to hate, we
> should lose the very spring of thought and action.
> Life would turn to a stagnant pool, were it not
> ruffled by the jarring interests, the unruly passions, of men.

He backs up his claim with examples relevant to his time and place, mentioning the enthusiastic crowds that gather at public executions, the gleeful persecution of witches, the annual burning of Guy Fawkes effigies, and various other ways that British citizens enthusiastically rallied around a common enemy. If he were writing today, he might have cited the "unruly passions" that American or European football fans focus on the opposing team, the attack ads and exaggerated claims that have become the staple of national and local elections, or the ways in which we (and our media spokespeople) turn on disgraced celebrities.

Hazlitt is provoking the reader, suggesting that we are not as free of antipathy as we like to believe, but he is also plumbing the depths of human nature, showing how the hatred of something or someone, often something or someone merely symbolic, can be pleasurable, and claiming that such ill feeling is an essential part of our character.

I won't go on to quote any more of Hazlitt's stimulating essay, though it is tempting to do so, because Hazlitt, despite his archaic diction, has a great gift for the fiery, passionate sentence. (Should you want to read more, though, let me pause here to point out that many classic essays, now well beyond their copyright dates, are available in full text online through Project Gutenberg, www.gutenberg.org, or the excellent essay resource Web site Quotidiana, www. quotidiana.org.)

I will, however, share Hazlitt's final words—the man has a subtle sense of humor, it turns out, despite his exaggerated zeal—where he finally runs out of targets and turns it all in on himself:

> Seeing all this as I do, and unravelling the web of human life into its various threads of meanness, spite, cowardice, want of feeling, and want of understanding, of indifference towards others, and ignorance of ourselves ... have I not reason to hate and to despise myself? Indeed I do; and chiefly for not having hated and despised the world enough.

 WRITING EXERCISE: ON THE PLEASURE OF _____

Two words that one wouldn't naturally put together, *hating* and *pleasure*, form the heart of Hazlitt's essay and provide a straightforward springboard for conflict. What else can you plug into that phrase, "On the Pleasure of _____," that might encourage the reader to keep turning the pages, just to see what you have to say?

You can be serious, as Hazlitt is for the most part, or you can have fun with this exercise. But your claim must incite initial skepticism in the average reader. ("On the Pleasure of a Sore Throat?")

Two suggestions:

1. You will need to back up your provocative title with tangible examples, as Hazlitt certainly did.

And

2. No one wants to merely be lectured at, so if you are claiming some flaw in the human character, it usually works best to expose your own complicity.

PUT THOUGHT INTO ACTION

Hazlitt had his vigorous opinions, but some folks go even further, taking their vigorous opinions and putting them into action. Henry David Thoreau spent a night in jail because he refused to pay his taxes in opposition to the Mexican-American War and slavery, and that defiant act resulted in the classic work *Civil Disobedience*.

Similarly, wanting to make a point about simplicity, technology, and the effects of societal "progress" on nature and man, Thoreau moved for two years to a cabin, near Walden Pond, and from that experience he created the still-celebrated *Walden; or, Life in the Woods*.

Here is his central claim:

> I see young men, my townsmen, whose misfortune it is to have inherited farms, houses, barns, cattle, and farming tools; for these are more easily acquired than got rid of. Better if they had been born in the open pasture and suckled by a wolf, that they might have seen with clearer eyes what field they were called to labor in. ... How many a poor immortal soul

have I met well nigh crushed and smothered under
its load, creeping down the road of life, pushing before it a barn seventy-five feet by forty, its Augean
stables never cleansed and one hundred acres of
land, tillage, mowing, pasture, and wood-lot! ... The
better part of the man is soon ploughed into the
soil for compost ... It is a fool's life, as they will find
when they get to the end of it, if not before.

Tough words, indeed, and still remarkable in their decisive opposition to the widespread notion that hard work leads to financial wealth, a big home, and ultimate happiness. Like Hazlitt, Thoreau knew that feeble claims and hesitant opinions were not going to gain a reader's attention.

The two years spent near Walden Pond allowed Thoreau to illustrate his ideas and gave him plenty of material, whether from his daily walks or his various encounters with the machinery of progress. His lifestyle was in conflict with societal forces, and his writing couldn't help but to reflect the conflict.

This form of participatory essaying lives on today, of course, when writers plunge themselves into their subject matter and test out their theories. You don't need to move into the woods for two years; it might be as simple as adopting a new habit, like stopping to talk to folks on your busy commute to work, buying only locally raised meats and vegetables, or turning off the Internet for a week.

The reader has to trust you a bit if you are willing to "not just talk the talk but walk the walk."

The Hot Winds That Blow

Not all conflict is based on philosophical or political disagreement, of course.

Look, for instance, at the opening to Joan Didion's essay, "The Santa Ana," from her wonderful collection, *Slouching Towards Bethlehem*:

> There is something uneasy in the Los Angeles air this afternoon, some unnatural stillness, some tension. What it means is that tonight a Santa Ana will begin to blow, a hot wind from the northeast whining down through the Cajon and San Gorgonio Passes, blowing up sand storms out along Route 66, drying the hills and the nerves to flash point.

Didion begins with the weather, but notice that one word: nerves. Soon enough in her essay she is talking about the human toll of the wind, how the eerie silence and intense heat cause people to act strangely, fearfully, sometimes violently.

She quotes detective novelist Raymond Chandler (author of *Farewell, My Lovely* and *The Big Sleep*):

> On nights like that, every booze party ends in a fight. Meek little wives feel the edge of the carving knife and study their husbands' necks. Anything can happen.

Her natural conflict—the weather—is the glue that holds her essay together, but within the frame she can explore any number of fascinating human stories, including her own reactions to the Santa Ana.

Her final sentence:

> The wind shows us how close to the edge we are.

Look Inward

Another of Didion's exquisite essays, "In Bed," attempts in just under 1,500 words to explain the intense sting, disorientation, and disruption of severe migraine headaches to those who have never had them.

Though the description can be excruciating, just like the pain itself, what fascinates me most about this essay is near the conclusion, when she writes:

> And I have learned now to live with it, learned when to expect it, how to outwit it, even how to regard it, when it does come, as more friend than lodger. We have reached a certain understanding, my migraine and I.

That understanding is what drives the essay.

 ## WRITING EXERCISE: ALMOST IMPOSSIBLE

You've heard certainly, perhaps spoken yourself, the words, "Oh, it is almost impossible to put into words how I feel right now." People say this about certain tragedies and disappointments, about the first throes of love, about some hilarious spontaneous moment, about the feelings a new father has when first holding his infant daughter.

There's nothing at all wrong with that common expression—"Oh, it is almost impossible to put into words"—*unless* you are a writer, in which case you simply cannot hide behind that excuse. It is your job as writer to take the most difficult experience and bring it alive, in detail, for readers who have not had that same experience. Didion does this, in attempting to explain her migraines.

What in your experience do you find "almost impossible" to explain?

Almost impossible means possible, though difficult.
You might as well start trying now.

MY ASSAY: WHEREIN THE AUTHOR ATTEMPTS TO FOLLOW HIS OWN ADVICE

Yes, I'm being a bit of a provocateur in my essay about walking and Boca Raton. I mean, after all, I *do* own a car, and I fully understand why so many of us need to use one. But I'm almost being honest: I often leave my car in the driveway and walk to work, and I'm glad to have formed this habit.

It saddens me how seldom people walk anymore, and I do worry about the impact our traffic-snarled culture has on both the community and the individual. I'm a bit like Thoreau, in that way, and while researching the examples used in this chapter, I serendipitously came across a lecture Thoreau gave later in his life, one that was published posthumously with the simple title, "Walking."

Let me quote briefly:

> I have met with but one or two persons in the course of my life who understood the art of Walking, that is, of taking walks—who had a genius, so to speak, for *sauntering*, which word is beautifully derived "from idle people who roved about the country, in the Middle Ages, and asked charity, under pretense of going *a la Sainte Terre*," to the Holy Land, till the children exclaimed, "There goes a *Sainte-Terrer*," a Saunterer, a Holy-Lander. They who never go to the Holy Land in their walks, as they pretend, are indeed mere idlers and vagabonds; but they who do go there are saunterers in the good sense, such as I mean.

Finding this passage has led me to make two changes in my essay-in-progress. The first is that I am breaking up the various sections of the essay with quotes from Thoreau's lecture, in much the same way that Montaigne peppered his essays with quotes from Virgil and Cicero.

The second change is that my essay is no longer titled "On Foot." I'm going with a more intriguing title, I think:

"Of Idle People Who Rove About."

We'll see where that leads.

OPPOSING IDEAS

The test of a first-rate intelligence is the ability to hold two or three opposing ideas in mind at the same time and still write elegant, detail-filled, fiery sentences.

Essayists don't have all the answers.

If they did, there would be no reason to write.

A CLOSER LOOK:
"AH, WILDERNESS!"

BY DINTY W. MOORE

A few chapters back, I offered a closer look at Agnes Repplier's essay "Leisure," and tried to illustrate what she was saying, how she employed the various expectations of essay-writing in her time, and suggested why she might have moved from point to point as she did.

I'm going to try it again with another essay, but this time I'll need to engage in far less speculation, since the essay is one that I wrote myself. It first appeared in an excellent literary magazine, *Arts & Letters: Journal of Contemporary Culture.*

The essay is a sort of hybrid between travel and nature writing, but in truth, I am essentially writing an essay of conflict and being a bit of a provocateur. Just as Repplier used many of her contemporary essayists and literary forerunners to underline her points—or as counterpoints against which she could argue—I use one writer, the respected essayist Rebecca Solnit, as my foil.

Full disclosure: I am a fan of Solnit's work across many genres—nature writing, political writing, technology writing—but I'm no fan in this essay. Here, I question not just Solnit's point-of-view on the Rio Grande River, but a disturbing trend I saw throughout much of the environmental movement. My essay would come off as wishy-washy, I'm sure, if I spent too much time talking about where I agree with Solnit or how fine a writer she is. In this essay, I focus my viewpoint on one of Solnit's essays, my own experience, and how I see things far differently.

But enough explanation. Here's my essay.

AH, WILDERNESS! HUMANS, HAWKS, AND ENVIRONMENTAL CORRECTNESS ON THE MUDDY RIO GRANDE BY DINTY W. MOORE

"You *can* steer, can't you?"

The question comes from Annie, a wiry, energetic woman of about fifty, with graying hair, dark eyes, a craggy face that belies countless hours under the sun. She wears Teva water shoes, neoprene bike shorts, black rowing gloves. I am here to relax, but clearly she is all business.

"Well, can you?"

Thirteen of us—three guides and ten paying customers—stand on the Texas side of the Rio Grande, just east of Big Bend National Park, about to launch eight canoes. The canoes sit low in the water, laden with tents, poles, food, paddles, pots, pans, stoves, water jugs, and a cumbrous portable toilet we will come to call "The Groaner."

In their wisdom, the guides have paired Annie and I together, but having sized me up in my old tennis sneakers, cheap t-shirt, and denim shorts, she seems not so sure. Steering a canoe is a dicey prospect under any circumstance, given the vagaries of water and wind; but in whitewater, steering can be life or death. Annie has reason to be cautious.

"You *do* have a draw stroke, right?" She is sensing my hesitation. "You *do* know how to read water?"

The simple answer is "yes," but the Rio Grande is capricious; a swirling mess of brown river, fast-moving and sided by high canyon and undercut rock. I *do* know a bit about steering a canoe, though not enough that Annie's aggressive questioning doesn't immediately make me forget it all.

The pairing remains, because the guides don't want to hear dissent. Worse yet, from Annie's perspective, I am awarded the stern, where the course is set and corrections made. The canoe's rear seat falls to me not because of gender or expertise, but because I outweigh Annie dramatically.

She reluctantly takes the bow, and one by one, the guides push the eight canoes into the swift current. When it is our turn, Annie commences paddling, paddling with immense effort, paddling at a rate easily three-times more vigorous than the bow paddler in any of the other five tandem boats. She paddles as if her very life depends on it, as if I have already announced loudly my plans to steer the canoe into the first dangerous hole I can find.

A QUICK INTERRUPTION here. What I am up to above is first of all to make the setting interesting. That's easy, of course, since we are taking canoes down a dangerous river, but I still need, as writer, to make the readers feel as if they are seeing, hearing, smelling, tasting, and touching the experience, as best as I can do in words.

Aside from orienting the reader so that the rest of my essay makes sense, I am introducing characters who will recur throughout. Annie, of course, my boat-mate on this first morning, is the most important. She is colorful, and as you will see later, she comes to embody the conflict I am about to frame between my own experience and the Rebecca Solnit essay I will soon quote.

Now, back to the action (and a flashback):

The evening before, thirteen of us meet in a motel in Odessa, Texas, home of the world's largest jackrabbit statue. We spend the following morning squeezed into a long blue Nantahala Outdoor Center van, riding across the endless flatness of the Permian Basin, all oil fields and dried-out ranches. We drop down through Fort Stockton, Marathon, past the Tinaja Mountains, before we find the unmarked road to our river put-in, at Heath Canyon Ranch.

Aside from Annie, the guests on this trip include a pair of retired Vermont schoolteachers; a Bermuda physician named Thomas and his birdwatching British wife, Lu; Fiona, a young pharmaceutical saleswoman; two other doctors, both traveling solo; Bill, a retired engineer; and me. Both of the American doctors are named Dave, and so earn the quick nicknames Tall Doctor Dave and Bearded Doctor Dave.

To amuse ourselves during our lengthy van ride to the put-in, we speculate on what the trip might bring. Tall Doctor Dave can do better than speculate, however; he is a Sierra Club member, and the environmentalist group's magazine features an article on the stretch of river we will soon be travelling. He has brought the article, "Texas on My Mind: Mexico on My Right," and reads us snippets. Author Rebecca Solnit describes our destination as "a slow-moving opaque soup with the occasional clot of foam floating atop it."

In the van, we wince.

In another section, Solnit warns that we will be bobbing through "just about every type of pollution imaginable, including radioactive sediments, industrial toxins, mine wastes, agricultural runoff, erosion caused by mining and logging, and improperly treated sewage."

We wince again, more noticeably this time. Tall Doctor Dave confesses that he almost cancelled the trip and sacrificed his deposit when the magazine arrived in his mailbox, but he really needed a week away from the operating room.

Finally, Solnit writes that the Rio Grande "annually dries up altogether at four points and runs perilously low elsewhere," and details how, because of upstream agricultural diversion, there was barely even enough water for her raft trip to pass through the lower canyons, our destination. She eventually managed to drag her raft out, but leaves the distinct impression that the next party to boat through might get stuck for all time.

The guides mumble something about Sierra Club negativity, but for the most part the van ride ends in silence.

Saturday afternoon, on the river, paddling like a demon just to keep up with Annie, I see no clots of foam, just lots of cool, quick mud-colored water. The sky is glassy blue, the air sweet smelling, the cliffs gorgeous, and the *Sierra* article is forgotten.

Our first campsite, Borland Canyon, is only five miles off, and with Annie's windmill strokes, we are there in no time. We camp on the Texas side, and at sundown are treated to a light show somewhere south in the Chihuahuan Desert. I have never seen lightning quite like this before; sharp blazing bolts running flat along the horizon, as if the sky itself has been turned on its side.

We finish our evening meal and bed down, then brace for the arrival of the torrential rains that follow the lightning. The storm lasts only ten minutes, but for the duration my tent feels as if it might lift up into the sky.

Morning, though, comes with sunshine, chirping birds, the sound of our lead guide, Fritz, shouting "Cawww-feeeee," in a Southern drawl more like a yodel than a yell. Fritz, a woman despite her nickname, will spend the week keeping us alerted to meals, changes in plans, imminent dangers, and bathroom arrangements. The latter will become quite complicated.

We stumble out of our various tents and take good-natured inventory of our aches and pains, and our survival. The brief encounter with nature's fury seems to pick up everyone's spirits.

Except Tall Doctor Dave, who emerges sopping wet. His gear is already a running joke—he came on the trip equipped with more rigging than an astronaut, it seems, most of it fluorescent orange or yellow, all of it dramatic on his 6'4" frame. Though we are paddling in extreme heat, he wears enough layered capilene and spandex that he would not look so out of place at a toxic chemical spill. He is a walking advertisement for REI, the catalog outfitter.

Despite his high-tech gear, though, it turns out that he somehow left Chicago without his fly—the taut, waterproof fabric square that stretches over a tent to deflect water away from the edges. As a result, the poor man slept much of the night in a puddle.

As most of us eat breakfast and remark on the beauty of the day, Tall Doctor Dave morosely shoves his drenched equipment and saturated sleeping bag into his gear sack.

"If we can get into camp early," Fritz promises, "and if the sun is still out, and if we can find some trees, that stuff should dry out just fine."

It seems like a lot of ifs, but our first full day on the river is filled with such beauty and interest, that even the lanky physician soon forgets to worry.

The immediate riverbank is overwhelmed with bamboo, but the hills on either side host a variety of desert flora—prickly pear cactus, barrel cactus, mesquite, acacia, and ocotillo. The river is a migratory route for birds, since there is very little water elsewhere in this desert region, so we see abundant great blue heron, cliff swallows, black phoebes, Swainson hawks. Lu, the birdwatcher, calls out the names for us.

The cliffs, and surrounding bluffs, grow more dramatic with each mile we cover. "Drink," Fritz shouts at regular intervals. "Keep drinking." Confined as we are between canyon walls, under a desert sun, we are baked goods—the real danger to our health and well being, given the gentleness of the rapids so far, is dehydration.

Annie, like the tall doctor, comes well-equipped. She wears a nylon water bag on her back, and drinks constantly from a hose that runs to her mouth. I, on the other hand, come poorly equipped, and am constantly filling, refilling, and dropping my empty Gatorade bottle into the mud on the bottom of the canoe, which always sends us off course, and sends Annie into a short panic.

In this fashion, we put seventeen miles behind us, then camp for our second night on a small, muddy ledge. The canyon walls cut us off from all but the faintest sunlight well before the sun actually sets, and since it is October, we light an early fire. Over a dinner of red beans and rice, we joke about Tall Doctor Dave's wet gear, about which paddling duo is slowest, which the most inept, and which duo bickers most constantly—the two Doctor Daves, it turns out, not Annie and me.

ANOTHER QUICK BREAK here. The detail about my dropping my water bottle in the canoe is true, but it also serves a purpose. I am willing to point out my own stupidity as readily as I am willing to poke fun at Tall Doctor Dave for his equipment mania or at Annie for her nervous paddling, and that, I hope, will keep the reader on my side.

No one likes a scold who has himself no sense of humor.

Tall Doctor Dave gives me his copy of the *Sierra* article, and that night, in my tent, I underline passages, wondering whether Rebecca Solnit could possibly have been on the same river we now travel.

Solnit bemoans "longhorn cattle grinding the riverbank into dust" and occasionally washing up dead, "further compromising the river." She mentions possible "killer bees," though she sees none, and "acrid, gritty dust that would blow into every crack in a tent and across every open dish, and onto our exposed skin." Her raft washes aground every few paragraphs, something she blames on all the farmers upstream and their wanton irrigation. At Hot Springs Rapid, our destination for the next evening, she even manages to encounter armed men that she assumes are with the Mexican army.

Solnit, it appears, feels threatened every step of the way, whereas I have never seen such beauty in my life. The few longhorn cattle I see along the riverbank are handsome and welcome. To her, they are uninvited despoilers of the earth. The water on which we paddle is an opaque brown, from the mud, but I am nonetheless grateful for the water, for the heat, for the light dust, for all that I've seen on this first day.

I worried in the van when Tall Doctor Dave started reading the article, worried that the trip brochure promising wild and scenic wilderness was some scam. Now I'm worried about Solnit and her readers, and am more than willing to side with the guides and their terse dismissal of "Sierra negativism." I'm not sure what Solnit was looking for on her trip, but I doubt she and I came looking for the same thing.

This apparent contradiction in those most committed to environmentalism has been noted before—the very experience of nature, the deep calm and solid centeredness that comes from being in the desert, on the shore, in the forest, is often not available to them, because they are perpetually anxious. As stewards of our planetary survival, they sacrifice any opportunity they ever had of enjoying the nature they want to protect.

At one point, Solnit worries in print about the Sierra Blanca nuclear-waste dump. The proposed facility is not even open at the time she is writing (nor is it now), and if it were to open, it would be several hundred miles upstream, and sixteen miles from the river. But, Solnit notes, the proximity of a possible earthquake fault line "would add to the radioactive threats to the Rio Grande."

If they build it, and if some waste escapes, and if there is an earthquake … well, it could happen. But I'm thinking, no wonder

Solnit's raft kept running aground—she came on her trip carrying a heavy load.

We enter the full force of the canyon on Monday, our third day on the river, and the view becomes truly breathtaking—one-thousand-foot sheer walls, castle-like bluffs, undercut canopies riddled with cliff swallow nests.

Equally striking is the absence of civilization. One other party—a couple in a canoe accompanied by a kayaker—pass by early that morning, but otherwise we seem to be the only humans on the river. Nor is there anyone visible on the adjoining land. The canyon walls make the riverbank, what there is of it, nearly inaccessible for about a seventy-mile stretch; that limits foot-travel, and it limits the canoe and raft traffic as well. Once into the lower canyons, you are in for the duration. It takes a commitment.

During the next few days, we will pass two, maybe three abandoned fishing camps, but see no one, just cows and birds. This remoteness from phones, e-mails, faxes, television, and other people, has a wonderfully calming effect. Even the guides eventually relax. We are, Fritz assures us, a "very low maintenance" group of guests.

Tall Doctor Dave encounters a new problem with his size-13 water sandals, but solves it by wrapping the sandals onto his feet with duct tape—fluorescent yellow duct tape. Fiona can barely stifle her giggles.

We stop around mid-day at a site the guides promise us is filled with fossils. "You can look at them, but you'll have to leave them where they are," Fritz instructs. A few trip members quote the ecologist's motto, "Leave nothing but your footprints, take nothing but your memories." Gary, one of the guides and a veteran of this canyon, lets us know that he has in fact seen the fossil field dwindle in the ten years or so that he has been making the trip. "They used to be everywhere," he says. "Now you really have to look."

And so we do, baking under the desert sun, turning over countless small sand-colored rocks. We find a few trilobite impressions, one or two fossilized clams, and a living scorpion or two.

We take nothing.

Or if anyone does, no one's telling.

Gradually, we enter deeper into the high canyon, and the river narrows, squeezing more water through an ever-tighter funnel of rock. As a result, the rapids become more potent, more dangerous.

And, as luck would have it, I am the first of the trip to be catapulted out of a boat. A miscalculation of mere inches and I shoot head over heels into Palmas Canyon rapid, a roiling mess of whitewater and rock. My boat, Annie at the bow, carries through the rapid without me. After feeling a blunt impact on my leg, I wash through as well, into a wide, shallow field of riffles and stone.

The guides are quick to throw ropes and shout lifesaving directives that I can't hear over the roar of the water, but none of this turns out to be necessary. Because the temporary widening has created a shallow area, I simply stand up and walk out. I earn a purple bruise the size of a bocce ball on my right thigh, but am otherwise unhurt.

My baptism becomes the source of much merriment, and we stop for lunch right where I fell, to mark the occasion. The unpacking of our lunch stores results, however, in a swarm of large, hovering, brown insects known as tarantula hawks.

They are wasps, actually, but very large wasps—roughly the size of small hummingbirds—and are given the striking name because their sting can paralyze a tarantula. The tarantula hawk will drag its immobilized victim away, and then deposit its eggs in the body of the living spider. Later, the wasp larva will hatch, and eat their way out.

Gruesome stuff, but they don't sting us. What they desperately want, instead, are our slices of ham. The next twenty minutes consist of swatting and griping, until I distract the group by accidentally discovering a different sort of insect, a rainbow grasshopper. This one is shaped like the grasshopper most of us know, but instead of a dull green or brown, it is covered in bright orange and blue mosaic tiles. It does not seem real; the colors are far too spectacular. But it is. The eyes move cautiously back and forth.

I bring the grasshopper into the group on the twig to which it has attached itself, and everyone crowds around. Solnit never mentioned this.

All of us on the trip have varying levels of experience—with rivers, and with wilderness. The guides, of course, have seen plenty, and many of the paying guests have taken two, even three trips a year for many years running. Often, during our meal breaks, they trade information on destinations and guide companies, thinking ahead to their next excursion.

For me, though, this is a first. I have never experienced so much wilderness in my life, never been so removed from civilization, never been so aware of my own smallness. I would often visit Niagara Falls as a kid, and though there is no denying the majesty of those particular rapids, they somehow weren't as impressive as this canyon. The difference, I decide, must be this: At Niagara Falls, we stand back and observe; here, on this trip, we have become part of the canyon, dependent on the flow of the river, subject to rock and weather, benefiting from the beauty at the same time that we are at risk from the remoteness and harsh geography. We have Igloo coolers, canned ham, bagged rice, and bottled water, so we aren't completely linked to the canyon's ecosystem, but for these seven days, we are beyond doubt at the canyon's mercy. The canyon is mighty.

I know what Solnit would say! The canyon may look pristine, majestic, and intact, but all the while small pollutants we can't see are destroying the delicate natural balance. Just because something looks magnificent doesn't mean it isn't being destroyed. Look at that footprint, over there! It's not just a footprint, it's erosion.

I appreciate her concern, but even a good thing can be carried too far.

Solnit acknowledges at one point in her article, in fact, that her trip companions, most of them Canadians, seem to be having quite the good time. "But then they were on vacation and determined to enjoy themselves," she writes.

What she doesn't seem to realize is that she seems just as determined not to enjoy herself.

I find one passage from Solnit's article almost laughable.

"After passing a herd of goats, I told my raft-mates the story of Esequiel Hernandez, the teenage goatherd who was shot in the back by U.S. Marines in Redford, Texas, not far from where we floated," she writes.

My God, I think—my last thought before I fall asleep—she must have been a hell of a fellow paddler on her raft trip. A real barrel of fun.

REMEMBER THE ADVICE of essayist Phillip Lopate: "Without conflict, your essay will drift into static mode, repeating your initial observation in a self-satisfied way. What gives an essay dynamism is the need to work out some problem, especially a problem that is not easily resolved."

As you can see, I am trying to work out my own internal conflict on the page, and to take the reader along with me on the journey of thought as well as on the journey of water and canoes. I am not arguing with Solnit's facts so much as I am arguing with her (in my opinion) negative point-of-view. And I'm not really arguing with Solnit, since who would really care about my opinion on her opinion?

Crafting the Personal Essay

Primarily, I am arguing with that portion of the environmental movement that feel as if they must paint the bleak-
est picture imaginable in order to get our attention. I am
concerned about those who love nature but have lost all
ability to enjoy it. What I hope gives my essay dynamism
is that I *agree* with the environmental movement, by and
large, but still find fault with their tactics and viewpoints.

I don't want to argue my point in abstract words and
intellectual concepts, however. That's academic writing,
and for most folks, boring to read. This is why I spend so
much time trying to make the reader feel as if they are
along on the Rio Grande with my canoe group. My aim is
to let the facts and details reveal the truth, and trust the
reader to interpret them clearly.

Wednesday, our fifth day together, the air turns cold, misty, gray,
and the paddling grows harder, thanks to a persistent upstream
wind. The trip members grow silent; even the guides recede into their
thoughts, right down to the vigilant Fritz, who for the first few days
would ask "is there anything you need" every twenty minutes.

The weather is surely a factor in our mood, but I think the
"canyon effect" becomes part of it as well. None of us feels quite
so significant as we did in our civilized lives. Our verbal clever-
ness doesn't seem quite so important to share. Who we are, what
we own, our job titles—all of these are fairly irrelevant. Our
perspective on nature has shifted, but more significantly, so has
our perspective on our selves. What we now see, I think, is closer
to the truth of the matter.

Only Thomas and Lu remain a team for the full seven days. The
rest of us play musical canoes every day or so, switching paddling
partners, trying out new seats, new chemistry. Annie paddles

now with Gary, one of the guides, and they quickly push out to the lead. Bearded Doctor Dave and I team up, and I'm finally switched to the bow, which affords a nicer view.

This day of dreary weather also brings a series of impassable rapids, or impassable at least in full boats with mid-level paddlers. To get by, we 'line' the boats, which means we stretch out along the rocky bank, brace ourselves against boulders to resist the rushing current, and pull the canoes along one by one, passing them from hand to hand, sometimes hoisting them over rocks too narrow for them to pass through. This is the most dangerous work of the trip. We must take care that the canoes don't come up the line too fast, pinning someone against the rocks, breaking a limb, or worse, forcing one of us underwater where the danger of becoming trapped by the current is great.

After a bit more paddling, we knock off early at a spot called Burro Bluff, one of the highest points within a hundred mile range. Gunshot thunder is coming from somewhere. Deep as we are in the belly of the canyon, it is hard to tell from exactly where. After our tents are staked and gear stored away, we hike up to the Bluff, past creosote, prickly pear, all manner of thorny plant-life. It is a steep hike—better suited for burros, hence the name, than people—but we are promised a stunning vista.

It takes a good 45 minutes to pull ourselves up the crisscrossing trail, and the view down into the canyon is, indeed, amazing. On a clear day, Fritz tells us, we could see deep into Mexico as well, but the heavy overcast cuts off our view.

We are on the Bluff for no more than two minutes before Fritz realizes the thunder is not so distant, that the storm is close, and bearing right down upon us. "Get your asses down the hill," she shouts, not needing to explain. We are standing on the highest point anywhere near, and we are human lightning rods.

The run back down is a comic stumble, the small rocks catching under foot like ball-bearings, the cacti snagging and scratching, the wonderful view forgotten.

The canyon rules all.

I *do* love the planet, though if Solnit were reading *this* essay as closely as I've read her essay, I suspect she would not think so. I am firmly against acid runoff, nuclear spillage, diverted rivers, and a host of other ecological evils. I believe that men, and women, would do better to cooperate with the Earth's ecosystem rather than run it into the ground. I think myself a reasonable man. But Solnit might lump me in with the irrigators, the lumber harvesters, the cattlemen, and all the others guilty of insensitive exploitation.

After all, I'm only human.

Which is precisely my problem with what she, and many of the eco-extremists—those who seem to get the most notice and thus have the biggest voice in the environmentalist movement— have to say. It too often sounds as if the human species is the only thing separating a contaminated planet from Eden. If the "cancer" we call human beings were to be cut away, they seem to imply, then all problems would somehow be solved. Whatever we do, however we interact with the environment is unnatural; whatever every other species does is as natural as rain. On this trip, we are hauling out not just our garbage and food waste, but our human waste as well, in that big tin box called the Groaner. Yet cows and goats and pigs and birds have been defecating along this river forever. They didn't seem to ruin anything. Tarantula hawks lay their eggs inside of live scorpions, so that their offspring can hatch and eat their way out, but that's natural. We, on the other hand, have to apologize for paddling up to the shoreline with our little tents, because we are flattening some grass, and maybe leaving a footprint or two.

What seems most pointless to me is the either/or nature of the argument. The Bible tells us that mankind has "dominion over the fish of the sea, and over the fowl of the air, and over the cattle, and over all the earth," and some interpret this to mean we can do as we please, when we please, without thought or moral center. The ecological extremists, on the other hand, seem to see us as the only species not entitled to interact with the Earth at all.

I don't see much of a future in either position.

Annie has made it clear to us that she shares some of Solnit's views, but with an added gender twist. "Back before the sky gods came, before history," she tells us during one of our snack breaks, "the earth was a matriarchy. There was no question where the power was—women were the ones who gave birth, so they had all the authority. Men had no idea if they even played a part in the birth process, so they had no sense of their own importance.

"But then women put men in charge of metallurgy, and everything changed," she explains. "That's why we're destroying the planet. The patriarchy is only concerned with maximum production. Men have no interest in nurturing, in preserving anything. All the patriarchy wants to do is produce more, more, more."

I COME RATHER close to sounding pompous above, in my sermon on the environmental movement, and then I criticize Annie a bit, using her own words. The essayist is allowed to have opinions of course, and conflict is a good thing, but I still don't want to come off as seeming superior.

I *don't* have all of the answers. Like the reader, I am figuring out what may be true and what may not as the trip progresses.

So as you see, I'm back to examining my own lack of perfection in the section that follows. And I mainly let the facts speak for themselves, before reaching my conclusion, where, in the tradition of the essay, I am still trying to assemble and examine my own best thoughts.

Crafting the Personal Essay

I am more than a little chagrined, then, when it is Annie who later catches me in an act of environmental misconduct.

So far we have camped on slabs of rock, on mud, on sand, once even on grass, but our Thursday evening campsite is a field of small stones. My ten-year-old daughter, Maria, collects stones, and when I wake up Friday, I can't resist the urge to gather a few of the more uniquely colored or patterned ones to bring her as my return gift. I am aware that this violates the strict "take nothing but your memories" rule, but my love for my daughter overtakes my conscience.

Annie, though, comes upon me as I collect a plastic baggie of pebbles. We are in a rock sea, billions of rocks washed down from the cliffs and unearthed by the river over thousands, maybe millions of years, but Annie catches on quickly to what I am doing, narrows her eyes.

Futilely, I try to convince her of my position. "A few rocks aren't going to make a difference," I say, pointing to the small stones all around.

That doesn't seem to impress her, so I lamely play a gender card: "They're for my daughter."

"You shouldn't take a thing," Annie answers with a chill. "Nothing."

This is the official position of the trip guides as well, but Fritz and her crew have no interest in policing our gear. Thomas and Lu, in fact, have for the last day or so been lifting rocks the size of footballs into their canoe. They are building a fireplace back home, and explain to me that they like to use rocks from each of their many adventure travel trips as architectural accents. Fritz says, "You really shouldn't do that" at one point, but otherwise lets the infraction slide. I don't know if Annie has said anything to them or not.

Later, Bearded Doctor Dave shares his own views of nature.

"Oh, these environmentalists are worrying for no reason," he says cheerfully. "We aren't going to destroy the planet. Nature always takes care of herself. When we get too many people around here, when things get too bad, nature will intervene."

"How?" I ask.

"Plague," he answers dispassionately. "It is only a matter of time before the planet is hit with its next widescale de-population. There are viruses out there we don't know about yet. Nature cleans its own house."

He is a physician, so we listen closely.

Moments later, Lu, reflecting on the imminent end of our trip, says, "My, we have been out of touch for so long. There are people out there wondering if we are still alive."

"We should be wondering if they are still alive," Bearded Doctor Dave answers quickly. "It's more dangerous in their world with all the car accidents, shootings, muggings, bombings, than it is out here. Why do you even assume at this point that your loved ones back home are still alive?"

We paddle the rest of the day with little said between us.

It has come down to this:

Rebecca Solnit is convinced that we are marring the planet willfully and with malice. Bearded Doctor Dave, it turns out, shares her views in his own odd way, but is instead focused on the ecosystem's coming revenge, the quiet shy planet striking back with a fury. Annie agrees with Solnit, and in addition, is pretty sure I'm one of the worst offenders. Thomas and Lu are collecting stones for their fireplace, and taking it all in stride. We are, all of us on the trip, dirty, tired, cold, scratched, and bruised, and as best as I can tell, the river is doing just fine. No one has seen a single clot of toxic foam.

We have met nature, debated our place in it, and found little common ground.

As for me, I don't object to using a big tin box for a toilet, and I even take my turn carrying the heavy receptacle on and off the canoe each day; and I don't mind carrying away all of our trash, right down to straining out the few grains of rice that fall into our dishwater when we do the pots and pans; I even follow the rule to bag up my apple cores, though I still contend the wildlife would have been more grateful had we left them. I don't mind any of it, really, but I object to the implication that we somehow don't belong, that our every step is unnatural and unwelcome.

As careful as we are, the fact remains that at each of our seven campsites we have squashed some bugs, flattened some plants, inadvertently knocked the needles off a few cacti, and eroded a bit of soil off the muddy banks as we scrambled up with our considerable gear. Do I have to feel horrible about this?

A friend of mine, an Appalachian hiker, has explained to me that anti-environmentalists are guilty of exaggerating the environmentalist position, that the entire environmental movement is being tarred with an eco-extremist brush to make the environmentalists' views easier to dismiss.

This is an old tactic, and I'm sure he is right. I don't mean to contribute to this distortion, but I have Solnit's article in front of me; I'm not making it up. And Annie really said those things. And I gave those rocks to my daughter, and still feel vaguely uneasy about whether I did the right or wrong thing.

My behavior has not been blameless, maybe, but it hasn't been so bad. Yes, I believe in the beauty and importance of the environment, and I believe in protecting it. But I'd also like to be a part of it. Call it selfish if you will, but I'd be quicker to support the preservation of an ecosystem that includes me as a regular member.

I didn't visit the river in a bulldozer, after all.

I came by canoe.

WRITING THE
SPIRITUAL ESSAY

"I honestly think in order to be a writer, you have to learn to be reverent. If not, why are you writing? Why are you here?"

—Anne Lamott

If the essayist's primary charge is to dive headlong into the uncertainty, it is no wonder that writing about spiritual matters has always been front and center in the personal essay tradition.

The Confessions of St. Augustine, written in the fifth century by a Christian bishop and theologian, may indeed be the world's first memoir, and the truth is that all of these centuries later, the book remains powerful and startling.

Why?

Because Augustine was honest. He didn't claim that his Christian beliefs were uncomplicated or that he fully understood every difficult aspect of his faith. He went straight to the doubt and contradictions.

The spiritual memoir may exist within a specific religious tradition—Judaic, Islamic, Sufic, Hindu, Christian, Zoroastrian—or it may be rooted entirely outside of organized religion. There are, in fact, spiritual writings from atheists and agnostics, from those who embrace New Age philosophies, and from those so uncertain of their basic beliefs that they have no idea where to place themselves.

What unites the spiritual essay, however, is the quest to explore life's basic mysteries: Is there a God (or Higher Power, or unexplained force that knits the universe together)? How do we know? What should we do with our doubt or certainty about what this God or power expects of us? If we are to live our beliefs, what is the proper way to act?

Philip Zaleski, editor of the annual *Best American Spiritual Writing* anthology, has defined the genre in a similar fashion, saying that spiritual writing "deals with the bedrock of human existence—why we are here, where we are going, and how we can comport ourselves with dignity along the way."

All that is needed to write a spiritual essay is honest curiosity about the questions that surround us. Speaking for myself, I can't imagine how anyone could not have that curiosity and some measure of uncertainty. Faith, by definition, means we don't know for sure.

But perhaps there are those people who feel one hundred percent certain.

Well, then, let me say this:

If you feel altogether sure that *every* question and mystery can be answered by following the teachings of a particular religious tradition, or, alternately, if you are steadfast and entirely secure in your atheism, then enjoy the benefits of your certainty, sleep well at night, use your confidence to do good in the world, and don't bother tackling the spiritual essay.

If you are *conflicted*, however …

Ah, that essay is just waiting to be written.

A Note on Spiritual Conflict

Understand that the spiritual essay is not meant to be a forum to attack the beliefs of others. The conflict within a spiritual essay is not between different religious traditions, alternate interpretations of scripture, or competing opinions on which faith is the one true faith. The conflict of the spiritual essay is internal. Most often, it has to do with our inability to be sure of what our spiritual convictions demand of us or with our failure to live up to those expectations given our clearly imperfect human nature.

I was raised Catholic, and attended Catholic schools straight through to the end of high school, back in the old days when nuns wore exotic black habits and the parish priest ran not only the school but the neighborhood as well. My second book, *The Accidental Buddhist: Mindfulness, Enlightenment, and Sitting Still,* was an extended spiritual essay examining how I eventually fell away from the teachings of the Catholic Church and found myself more attracted to Zen meditation and Buddhist mindfulness.

Buddhism—more philosophy than religion—is 2,500-years-old, and much of what we know as Buddhism today is deeply intertwined with Asian cultures, so a good portion of the book explored the awkward fit between this different way of thinking and twentieth-century America in the age of the cell phone, the Internet, and instant gratification. The book focused as well, however, on my own efforts and failures attempting to live a mindful lifestyle and embrace the basic teachings.

I didn't have to disprove the tradition of Catholicism to make my point. In fact, many portions of the book explore my journey back into my Catholic past, including time spent with a Jesuit priest who was also a Zen teacher. I ended up finding a great deal in common between the roots of my Catholic tradition and the basic tenets of Buddhism, and hope that I succeeded in treating both belief systems with respect.

Writing that book taught me much—about writing, of course, because every new piece of writing attempted, even if it doesn't work out, teaches us something about writing— but also about myself and how I want to act in the world. That's the true power of spiritual writing. It is not just about reaching others, though giving comfort and inspiration to others can certainly be counted among the blessings. Writing the spiritual essay is about discovering parts of your own self.

Three Quick Tips

- Start small. Don't attempt to answer all of the great religious mysteries your first time out. How did we get here? What happens after we die? There are one-thousand-page books that explore those questions without ever reaching firm resolution. Look for a smaller piece of the puzzle of life, and start exploring there.

- As with every essay genre we've discussed so far in this book, specific stories from your past or examples from the lives of those you know well help to illustrate either your confusion or the tentative realizations you are *assaying*. These scenes and stories can be far more convincing than abstract explanations and are much more compelling on the page.

- Read some contemporary spiritual essays to see how the genre has changed since St. Augustine wrote his weighty tomes. Great essays from a myriad of traditions can be found at *Beliefnet* (www.beliefnet.com).

YOUR SPIRITUAL ESSAY

These prompts, remember, are here merely to get you started. They are not strict guidelines or rigid maps. If one of these prompts seems to be directing you down a certain path, but your instincts suggest a different path branching off to the left a bit or to the right, follow your instincts. The goal is to discover your spiritual questions, not mine:

1. How do you pray? Do you kneel down beside the bed the way a child is taught to do it? Do you fold your hands? Do you even use words? Can action be prayer? How about meditation?

2. If you knew for sure that there was no Heaven or Hell, would you act differently in your life?

3. What does "sacred" mean to you?

4. Write a brief essay entitled "My First Sin." You needn't define sin the way a priest or rabbi might define it. The definition is up to you.

5. Author Tobias Wolff suggests that writing the personal essay calls on us to "surrender for a time our pose of unshakable rectitude, and to admit that we are, despite our best intentions, subject to all manner of doubt and weakness and foolish wanting." Where are you guilty of acting righteous and sure in your life when in truth you are probably less certain than you seem to others?

6. Do cats and dogs have souls?

7. Rainer Maria Rilke offers this advice: "Be patient toward all that is unsolved in your heart and to try

to love the questions themselves like locked rooms and like books that are written in a very foreign tongue." What is unsolved in your heart? What questions have you locked away?

8. Have you had a spiritually significant moment, a moment of transformation, in church or perhaps during a time that you were very ill or during a long walk along the beach in winter? If so, write about that moment, but don't tell us what you realized or decided in that moment, instead tell us how it felt: Was there a sensation in your nervous system, a tingling on your skin, a chill, or a fever? Did your vision change? Did you hear something? Where were you, what objects surrounded you, what was the weather like that day? Describe only the physical manifestations of your spiritual epiphany.

9. Write about your parents' faith. Were they devout, or did it sometimes seem as if they were just going through the motions? Did their faith or strongest beliefs change as they grew older?

10. You've heard the expression "charity begins at home." What does that mean to you? Is being charitable to others part of your spiritual beliefs?

11. Perhaps, with respect, explore a holiday or ritual that is not part of your tradition. What is the Mexican ritual of *Dia de los Muertos* all about? Is it just alien to you, or do you wish your church had something so colorful? Would you rather be baptized in a river or in the back of the church with just a splash of water? If you are not Jewish, which of

the various Jewish holidays would you like to learn more about? If you are Jewish, what don't you understand about Christmas?

12. Many religions have a tradition of sacred dance, but why stop there? Do you believe there is such a thing as sacred gardening? Sacred walking? Sacred child rearing?

13. My good friend Diana lives in an old Methodist church. The cross has been taken down from the roof, and the various religious artifacts were claimed by other parishes, but there are still pews, still a platform where the altar once stood, and still a churchlike feel in the interior. Could you ever live in a reconditioned church? Do you think people should be encouraged to recycle buildings in this way, or does it somehow seem wrong to you?

14. Other than your parents, who has influenced your beliefs the most?

WHO AM I TODAY?

"Without that strong personal presence, the essay doesn't quite exist; it becomes an article, a piece, or some other indefinable verbal construction."
—Joseph Epstein

I remember well the self-doubts of my early writing career, when I felt completely unsure that I could ever write anything that was worthy of notice or publication.

One particular evening a few decades back, firm in my memory even now, I turned toward my wife, Renita, and moaned, "Oh, I'm just so average. Your typical guy with the typical tedious problems. Who wants to hear my story?"

My wife closed the book she had been reading for a moment, and asked, "What do you mean?"

I whined some more, about an author who had just landed a big book deal. Ethnic memoirs were all the rage at that point in time and this writer had been raised by parents who once lived in Japanese internment camps. Then I complained a bit about another writer: Her father had been a diplomat, so she grew up all over the world, and at one point even survived a dangerous escape during a foreign *coup d'etat*.

"Me?" I whimpered. "My life is just about identical to every other Catholic white kid raised in the 1960s."

At this point, Renita, bless her generous heart, nodded, smiled, and said, "Well, then you should write about that."

And she was right.

I was undervaluing my own singular nature and experience: Each person, each life, is distinctive, even if you didn't grow up in a family of acrobats or spend ten years sleeping alongside lions on the African veldt. It is not what happens to us in our lives that makes us into writers; it is what we make out of what happens to us. It is our distinctive point-of-view.

This is true especially for the personal essay, since all that the essay really demands of the writer is to have an interesting mind, and, as Epstein reminds us in the quote that begins this chapter, a "strong personal presence."

WRITING EXERCISE: PLAIN VANILLA YOU

What makes you dull and uninteresting?

That may seem like exactly the wrong place to begin an essay, but consider that 99.4 percent of all readers also worry at some point, or all of the time, that they are dull and uninteresting, not worthy of notice, unimpressive. This sense of personal mediocrity is probably far worse in our current era, where celebrity news is tweeted at us every waking second.

So you never killed someone or escaped from a Thai prison, never married and then quickly divorced a movie star or turned up half-naked in a jittery video on YouTube.

So what? Good for you!

If you feel dull and unspectacular, the reader is already on your side.

Think a moment, as well, of how many of the truly extraordinary people with flashy lives that incite our deepest jealousy end up in scandal or rehab? I've had some scandal in my life, but you know what, almost nobody knows about it, because almost no one cares.

Maybe just being a regular sort of guy or gal has its advantages.

Explore your feelings about your own personal dullness and normalcy a while, on the page.

ON PERSONA

The concept of persona is crucially important for essayists to understand.

Though the personal essay is a form of nonfiction, and thus the self you bring to your essay should be an honest representation of who you are, we are in fact made of many selves: our happy self, our sad self, our indignant self, our skeptical self, our optimistic self, our worried self, our demanding self, our rascally self, and on and on and on. But in truth, if we attempt to bring all of these selves to every essay that we write, we run the risk of seeming so uncertain, so indecisive, that we merely confuse the reader.

Consistent and engaging personality on the page is often a case of choosing which "self" is speaking in a particular essay and dialing up the energy on that emotion or point of view. Henry David Thoreau likely had days when Walden Pond did *not* fill him with wonder and inspiration, but he knew enough to not share those tedious moments. They were beside the point. Or put it another way, dithering is best left to first drafts, and then carefully edited away.

The goal is not to deceive the reader, to pretend to be someone that you are not, but rather to partially isolate a part of who you are, the "you" that you are today, as you meditate on a particular subject, and sit down to write.

You heard the whiny and insecure me in the anecdote that opened this chapter, now listen to the firm and decisive me: Persona matters!

Here are a few examples of how other writers have tackled the question, "Who am I Today?"

Be Honest, But Clear

The slogan of the excellent literary journal *Creative Nonfiction* is "You just can't make this stuff up." The slogan is effective, I believe, because of its double meaning. One meaning is that the truth is often stranger than fiction. The second meaning reminds the writer that in nonfiction, you are not just making stuff up.

So don't fake it. Don't act all pious on the page if you are not in fact a devout person. Don't generate false outrage over something you don't care that much about. Don't be a hypocrite.

But you can highlight a *particular* trait, if it is in fact true to your nature, and shine a bright light upon it for a few pages, letting it take center stage.

Look at Robin Hemley's introduction to his essay, "No Pleasure But Meanness."

> I have a mean bone in my body. In fact, I think I have more than one mean bone. For instance, I hate people who smile all the time. It feels good to say that word, "hate," doesn't it? Would you like to try it? Say: "I hate people who ask rhetorical questions in essays that can't possibly be answered."

Hemley is being witty here, poking fun at himself and at his overuse of the rhetorical question. He is also signaling the reader that this essay will focus on that part of him that can be called "mean," or critical.

I happen to know the author of this essay, and he is a very likeable, extremely funny man. Yet he no doubt has his mean moments, times when the things that annoy him no doubt lead to testiness or sharp anger. We all have that side to us, I believe. Perhaps inspired by William Hazlitt's "On the Pleasure of Hating," Hemley is taking a moment in his own essay to explore that aspect of himself, closely and specifically.

The essay continues with the author lodging numerous complaints, against folks who smile too much in photographs, against the checkout clerk at Walmart, against his kindergarten teacher, and though Hemley continues to leaven his bread of anger with humor and occasional winks to the reader, he does reveal a part of who he is honestly, clearly, and with interest.

Another good example might be Joan Didion, one of the finest essayists of all time in my opinion. She begins her essay, "In the Islands," with these two sentences:

> I tell you this not as aimless revelation but because I want you to know, as you read me, precisely who I am and where I am and what is on my mind. I want you to understand exactly what you are getting: you are getting a woman who for some time now has felt radically separated from most of the ideas that seem to interest other people.

Well, you simply can't get much clearer, or more honest, than that.

You Are Universal

That slight aspect of your personality or fantasy life, or hidden world, that you think so odd, so peculiar, so weird, that you've kept it a secret your entire life, is most likely far more common than you think. We are all made of similar stuff, we human beings. Even our most closely guarded insecurities are often commonly held, though most individuals keep these parts of themselves so hidden that there is little chance to discover the commonality.

But writers are different. We *do* share. And along the way readers come to an understanding that we are all very much alike.

The French essayist Michel de Montaigne devotes much of his essay, "Of Repentance," to this notion of universality.

Consider these sentences:

> Others form man; I only report him: and repre-
> sent a particular one, ill fashioned enough, and
> whom, if I had to model him anew, I should cer-
> tainly make something else than what he is: but
> that's past recalling ... If the world find fault that
> I speak too much of myself, I find fault that they
> do not so much as think of themselves. But is it
> reason, that being so particular in my way of liv-
> ing, I should pretend to recommend myself to the
> public knowledge?

Here, Montaigne is addressing a bit of anticipated criticism. In modern parlance, that criticism might go like this: "Just who the heck do you think you are, Mr. Montaigne, to write about yourself all of the time? Shouldn't you confine your writings to the vaunted geniuses and holy persons of past ages, instead of focusing all of the time on your own unproven self?"

He goes on to say (in his now quite-dated syntax):

> I have this, at least, according to discipline, that
> never any man treated of a subject he better un-
> derstood and knew, than I what I have undertaken,
> and that in this I am the most understanding man

Crafting the Personal Essay

alive: secondly, that never any man penetrated far-
ther into his matter, nor better and more distinctly
sifted the parts and sequences of it, nor ever more
exactly and fully arrived at the end he proposed to
himself ... I speak truth, not so much as I would, but
as much as I dare; and I dare a little the more, as I
grow older; for, methinks, custom allows to age more
liberty of prating, and more indiscretion of talking
of a man's self.

Montaigne is answering his critics by asserting (in my words
now, not his): "Oh yeah, well let me tell you this much, buster.
What I know best is my own self, and I know my own self really
really well, because I'm willing to study this subject and truly
consider it in ways that others have not been willing to do. And
if what I find is that I'm not so bloody perfect, well then I'll tell
you that. Because I'm too old to waste time and hide behind
niceties. I'm looking for the truth."

Montaigne, underneath all of the complex sentences and
fancy language, is making a simple assertion. It is his belief
that if he captures a true portrait of himself, he will capture
something universal, something recognizable to everyone.

Or as he puts it, elsewhere in the same essay: "... every man
carries the entire form of human condition."

Choose Wisely

Memoirist Sue William Silverman often receives letters and
e-mail from readers, and recently she shared a fascinating reaction to some of the responses to her first two books, *Because I
Remember Terror, Father, I Remember You* and *Love Sick*.

Silverman's memoirs are deeply personal and honest about
events and behaviors in the author's past, and many of the notes

Silverman finds in her mailbox say, in so many words, "I feel as if I know you."

In response to this Silverman writes:

> Both memoirs frequently elicit this response ... even though both books are very different. What does Karen know about me? Marie? Karen knows what it was like for me to grow up in an incestuous family. Marie knows what it was like for me to recover from a sexual addiction. To Karen, the real me is one thing; to Marie, the real me is something, someone different. Even so, does this mean that *all* I am—as a writer and as a woman—is an incest survivor/sex addict? Is that it?

Silverman, of course, is far more than just that. She is a successful author, a respected teacher, a public speaker, a private person who has had countless challenges and experiences. Everything she has put into her memoirs is true, yes, but then again, neither of her books captures the entire person that she has been and that she is today.

Sometimes she herself wonders who this "Sue William Silverman" on the page really is, Silverman tells us, and she has reached the conclusion that readers are wrong to think that they know her:

> ... they know *something* about me, of course—but only what I choose to show in any given book or essay. It's as if, with each new piece I write, a different "me," or a different aspect of myself, is highlighted.

To make her point, she talks about an essay she is currently drafting, part of her collection-in-progress, *The Pat Boone Fan Club: My Life as a White Anglo-Saxon Jew*.

When writing about Pat Boone, for example, I had to show how, since my Jewish father had molested me, it made sense that I'd seek out an overtly Christian man as a father figure. But I touched upon this incestuous background as briefly as possible, while, at the same time, implementing a much more ironic voice than that of my memoir. In effect, I removed the dark gray mask I wore while writing the memoir, and, for the essay, slipped on one that had as many sparkles as the red-white-and-blue costume Pat Boone wears in his concerts.

Had Silverman the writer attempted to bring her whole identity—her family past, her sexual addiction—into everything she has ever written, she would likely keep writing the same book or same essay over and over, and no one grows as a writer by merely repeating past work. Silverman is smart enough to know that.

Make sure you remember this as well.

 ## WRITING EXERCISE: THE MYRIAD SELF

Who are you?

Fill in some of these blanks:

I am a _____ son/daughter.

I am a _____ husband/wife.

I am a _____ parent.

I am also a _____ parent.

I am a _____ eater.

I am a _____ friend.

I am also a _____ friend.

I am a _____-friend.

I am a _____ when confronted with direct criticism.

I am a _____ when offered warmth and love.

I am a _____, but most of my friends never suspect this about me.

Now start an essay that takes just one of the personas above and uses it as the "strong personal presence." Choose one more—but just one—and let it be the secondary "you" we meet on the page.

Let these two true parts of who you are represent you here, but don't attempt to cover the entirety of who you are as a person. It isn't wise, and it likely isn't possible.

A Bit of Sarcasm, Maybe?

Back in high school you were probably asked to read Jonathan Swift's "A Modest Proposal." Actually, the full title is "A Modest Proposal for preventing the children of poor people in Ireland, from being a burden on their parents or country, and for making them beneficial to the publick." You can see why it is often abbreviated.

Writing in 1729, Swift offers a tongue-in-cheek, so-straight-faced-as-to-be-almost-believable "proposal" for how to deal with the countless poor children in Ireland and turn them into "sound and useful members of the common-wealth."

He bemoans the growing numbers of these youngsters to be found on every street and corner, before slyly stating

> ... I have been assured by a very knowing American of my acquaintance in London, that a young healthy child well nursed, is, at a year old, a most delicious nourishing and wholesome food, whether stewed, roasted, baked, or boiled; and I make no doubt that it will equally serve in a *fricasie*, or a *ragoust*.

Swift goes on to lay out his plan for separating some of these children "to breed," while "the remaining hundred thousand should be put up for sale to good families," once they have been allowed to "suck plentifully in the last month, so as to render them plump, and fat for a good table."

He even offers some advice on cooking and portions:

> A child will make two dishes at an entertainment for friends, and when the family dines alone, the fore or hind quarter will make a reasonable dish, and seasoned with a little pepper or salt, will be very good boiled on the fourth day, especially in winter.

Yes, Swift is kidding, but not because he wants the reader to laugh. He is skewering his government's lack of action to care for the poor, and mocking the callous attitudes displayed by some in eighteenth-century British society. He is being highly sarcastic, to make his point.

That sarcasm, too, is a part of persona. Swift didn't believe that children should be cooked and quartered, nor did he usually talk or write this way, but on the particular day that he decided to write his "Modest Proposal," he chose to highlight and embrace his entirely sarcastic self.

MY ASSAY: WHEREIN THE AUTHOR ATTEMPTS TO FOLLOW HIS OWN ADVICE

I know full well that one of the reasons Boca Raton was so empty—the houses all shuttered, the front porches devoid of rocking chairs and chatting neighbors—was the fact that it is stinking hot in south Florida, even in early April. If I lived in Florida full-time, perhaps even I would fall into the same reclusive patterns that you heard me decry in the sections of

"Of Idle People Who Rove About" that I have shared so far. Air-conditioning is a wonderful invention and has no doubt saved lives.

But this is *my* essay, and the person speaking is the part of me that can be critical of others, and the part of me that truly loves walking, and the part of me that truly values my interactions with neighbors; and this is an area of the essay I perhaps need to flesh out, so the reader understands from where I come, and why I feel so strongly.

So I'm working up a section that begins like this:

> I live in a small college town in Appalachian Ohio, and often walk to work. It takes me forty-five minutes, which can be tiring at times, but the more I do it the quicker the time goes by. For a while, I worried that I could get more work done if I didn't spend 90 minutes walking to and from campus. But eventually I realized I did get more work done on the days that I walked, because I was sharper, clearer, had used some of the foot-time to sort the detritus from my brain and identify the daily to-do list that actually mattered. What I really like about walking to work is that I see people.

To make my point convincing, I think I'll have to get specific—what people, and why does bumping into neighbors and strangers feel so good to me? Can I re-create for the reader the experiences I have walking across my little town?

If I can capture that, the reader may be swayed. If not, I run the risk of just sounding cranky.

Yes, cranky is probably part of my persona as well, but not one that I want to dominate *this* essay.

THE VOICES INSIDE

Do you remember the story that I used to open this chapter, the one where I turn to my wife and bemoan my normal, uninteresting life? I've come to recognize that voice inside of myself, the part of me that wants to undercut my own belief in my own talent or potential. I don't know why that voice exists, but it does, seemingly in all of us who try to write. It is the voice that tells non-writers that they are not pretty enough, not loveable enough, or not smart enough to succeed in life. It is the voice that tells us that our work is dull, too derivative, corny, trite, ham-handed, or somehow below the line that makes writing worthy or of value.

Well, since we are focusing on persona in this chapter, let me take a minute to say that this is *one* part of your persona that you needn't honor or bring to the table when you sit down to write. Most writers—beginning and accomplished—are just too hard on themselves. I'll say more on this in a later chapter about writer's block, but for now, here's my best advice: Be hard on your sentences, be hard on your paragraphs, be ceaseless and unrelenting in your revisions, but stop questioning your ability to be a writer. If you put pen to paper, or put electronic words on the page, you *are* a writer. Let go of that worry and focus on how good a writer you can become.

One sure way to become as good a writer as you can become is to allow your *self* into the writing, to make room for that "strong personal presence."

Of course, it can sometimes be hard not to.

Listen to this advice from the poet, dramatist, and philosopher Johann Wolfgang von Goethe: "Every author in some way portrays himself in his works, even if it be against his will."

WRITING THE GASTRONOMICAL ESSAY

*"The primary requisite for writing well about food
is a good appetite."*

—A. J. Liebling

Hector's was the quintessential Italian-American neighborhood restaurant, with a separate "family" entrance that allowed ladies and children to enter without passing through the tavern at the front. The dining room itself was dark, with candles inside of red glass holders on each of the dozen or so tables, old photos of Italy on the walls, and paper tablecloths. There was nothing fancy about the place.

Luigi's, right across the street, had green-checked cotton tablecloths, but we were a Hector's family because my mother liked the bread, served with cold, square pats of butter, and she liked that the waitress, Patsy, remembered us whenever we came in.

Patsy's white hair was always gathered in the back, pinned into a tight bun. She wore large white shoes, with thick, white rubber heels.

After Patsy led us to our table, my mother would study her menu while I turned around in my chair to study the other diners. There were usually a few small family groupings, and one or two elderly folks eating alone.

I don't know why Mom even consulted the menu, because we always ordered spaghetti with meat sauce, and it was always piping hot, a blast of tomato-and-garlic-flavored steam coming up off the white plate. In fact, the reason I remember so many details, even now, is that I can recall that rich aroma as if it were yesterday.

The link between these early recollections and that steaming plate of noodles can in fact be explained by science. Researchers have long known of the link between odor, memory, and emotion, and have even found an anatomical basis. The primary olfactory cortex—where messages from the nerves in the nose are processed—links directly to the amygdala and the hippocampus, those parts of the brain which control the experience of emotion and the consolidation of memories.

Or in layman's terms, when I remember the smell of Hector's spaghetti with meat sauce, a floodgate of hidden memory opens.

The Role of Food in Just About Everything

We spend so much time thinking about food (or if we are dieting, trying not to think about it), that it's only natural we write about it as well.

Consider just how many childhood memories somehow attach to food. Our birthday reminiscences often connect to cake and ice cream, our holiday memories are attached to days of cooking and baking and eating, and, for some of us lucky enough, our coming home from school memories include special treats just out of the oven. If your family went camping or had a cabin, you probably recall cooking hot dogs on an open fire. Our recollections of a departed grandmother may be linked to the smell of boiling cabbage or pot roast with onions, and even memories of family funerals often include neighbors dropping by with casseroles and platters.

As adults, food often remains central as well, as a way to rejoice or console. Many people, myself included, find that when we are happy, we eat something special to celebrate, and when we are depressed, we allow ourselves some sort of treat in order to cheer ourselves up.

That's not good for our waistlines, but it *is* human nature.

Food is not just sustenance, then, it is a mood changer, an essential component of marking key events in our lives

Moreover, food is frequently representative of culture and identity.

"If there is a key to unlocking the culinary secrets of the Coleman family," author Henry Louis Gates writes, "it is that a slab of fatback or a cupful of bacon drippings or a couple of ham hocks and a long simmering time are absolutely essential to a well-cooked vegetable."

"Sunday" is a gem of an essay that reaches just past 400 words, but in that brief frame Gates mixes in African-American family ritual, the irony of segregated lunch counters, cultural differences in seasoning and vegetable preparation, his father's sharp humor, and a vivid listing of ingredients and dishes served, until, at the very end, his Aunt Marguerite says, "White people just can't cook good ... that's why they need to hire us."

Gates opens up his whole family and culture to us just by describing one meal.

Here are some tips and prompts to help get you writing about the role of food in your life and the life of your family and community.

Three Quick Tips

- A good food essay is not a restaurant review or a recipe (though you can certainly include one) or a mere catalogue of ingredients. Imagine your gastronomical adventure as more of a travel essay, a journey into an unusual location: Pay close attention to aroma, texture, taste, and color, but also let your mind wander a bit. Remember that Marcel Proust produced a 3,200 page novel, *Remembrance of Things Past*, from the simple recall of a French pastry.

- M. F. K. Fisher's 1942 book of food essays, *How to Cook a Wolf*, is chock-full of cooking tips, recipes, humor, and sumptuous description, but it is also firmly grounded in her skeptical outlook on politics and the wartime shortages of the time. Connect your essay on food with the events and ideas of the time and place—food in the middle-class American family of the 1960s is different than the food consumed by middle-class American families today, and part of that difference speaks to changes in values, customs, and economic realities.

- There is a reason that this chapter appears directly after the chapter titled "Who Am I Today?" If you are going to write about food, the strong personal presence you need to bring to the page is that part of you that adores cooking, absolutely loves shopping for unique ingredients, and goes weak in the knees when finding the perfectly ripe avocado. Highlight the side of your personality that absorbs well-prepared food in every way: taste, smell, texture, even the sound that comes with snapping the ends off of crisp green beans. That's the "you" that should be front and center this time around.

Your Gastronomical Essay

As always, these prompts are meant as suggestions. Let them lead you where they will, and *bon appetit*:

1. Describe your most memorable meal (good or bad). Describe the food but also the people who were there with you, the setting, the ambient sounds in the room, and how you felt before and after.

2. What was the best dish in your mother's repertoire? Did your father cook too? What was his signature dish?

3. Do the differences between these two dishes say something about your father and mother's personalities? Or something about the differences between men and women at that time?

4. What were some of the packaged food peculiarities in your family? Were there certain brand names you always used, or peculiar convenience foods that seemed wonderful back then and just plain odd when you think about them now?

5. Write about a time you visited your Aunt Dora in New Jersey or stayed for dinner with the family down the street and found yourself baffled by someone else's food choices. We tend as children to imagine that our family habits are "normal," until we get out in the world and see just how different

every family can be. What surprised you at someone else's table?

6. How old were you when you realized vegetables didn't have to be limp and tasteless?

7. Do you remember TV dinners, the old-fashioned kind that cooked in the oven, and the puff of steam when you pulled back the foil covering? How about TV tables?

8. Many of my childhood food memories revolve around specific brand names. For instance, the strict use of Hellman's mayonnaise in our house seemed almost as important as what church we attended. It would have been blasphemy to suggest using Miracle Whip. Did you family have any stringent brand-name loyalties?

9. Our travel memories almost always include unforgettable meals or unusual regional dishes, from the *tapas* of Spain to the gumbo of Louisiana. Have you had fascinating experiences with regional or national foods?

10. Visit your local farmer's market or gourmet grocery. Buy a vegetable you've never before prepared, and teach yourself to make something.

11. The appreciation of food is more than just eating, of course. Calvin Trillin, for instance, in his many witty New Yorker pieces, makes his search for exotic foods on the streets of New York every bit as interesting as the gastronomic delights he eventually finds. Though we live in a world of plastic wrap and

mega-groceries, we are still hunters and gatherers of a sort, are we not?

12. What was the most exotic food you ever tried to cook? Squid, maybe? This story would be good if you succeeded, but just as good (maybe better) if you totally failed.

13. If you had a staff of six chefs assisting you, all the time in the world, and all of the ingredients you could ever imagine, and were going to make a dinner to end all dinners for your very best friends and most cherished loved ones, what would the menu look like?

14. Food is love. Discuss.

WRITING THE HUMOROUS ESSAY

"It took me fifteen years to discover I had no talent for writing, but I couldn't give it up because by that time I was too famous."
—Robert Benchley

"You want a chair that makes you comfortable, isn't that right?"

My wife and I, blundering into a furniture showroom just slightly smaller than the state of Delaware, found ourselves ambushed by a chipmunk of a man. He was barely over five feet tall, his dark hair thinning in patches, and his robin's-egg-blue blazer as unstylish and unattractive as any blazer I've ever seen. But he had clear, direct eyes, and an irresistible slow, spreading smile.

That was *my* initial assessment. What *he* saw, perhaps, were two shy, middle-class pigeons with "easy sale" tattooed on their foreheads.

The gentleman introduced himself as Howie, "your furniture consultant for today," pumped my hand and winked at my spouse. "You want a comfortable chair, yes? One you can sit in and relax?"

He was, it seemed, not just a furniture consultant but a mind reader as well, having intuited by my mere explanation "we're looking at chairs" that Renita and I had absolutely no interest in an uncomfortable chair that made us squirm and kept us endlessly tense.

"I'm going to take you around," he announced, a trace of Brooklyn in his voice. "We have over three-thousand chairs in our showroom today. I'm going to show you all of them."

Howie was a bit pushy, slick, and peculiar, and yet it was somehow impossible not to like the man. His gaze was warm and neighborly. He had that slow, spreading smile. I don't understand how it all works, but within moments of entering Howie's magnetic field, I wanted to befriend him. I wanted him to be my grandfather, even though I suspected that if he *were* my grandfather, the piece of butterscotch candy he would pull for me from his pocket would be ten-years-old and lint covered.

Yes, I would love him anyway.

Howie told me he was the top salesperson for the entire Mid-Atlantic region. I didn't doubt him for one second.

A few minutes into our hunt, when I rejected the whole category of chair that I call "marshmallow-puffy recliner," Howie turned, extended his hands palms upward and promised: "I'm not going to make you buy something you don't want."

It didn't make sense to me at the time—why ever would I buy something I didn't want?—but after thirty minutes with Howie, I understood that I might have done just that. He had that certain power.

We passed through the giant circular showroom, rejecting chair after chair. "You like this one?" Howie would ask. He would pause then, study my face, and before I could form an answer, he would say, "Of course not, I knew you wouldn't!"

Along the way, my wife and I let it slip that we had just moved into town. Howie, it turned out, was about to leave, for a better furniture consultant job down South. We mentioned our small, untrainable pup.

"You have small dog? *I* have a small dog!"

Howie could not have been more delighted had I just revealed that I was his long lost son, orphaned at birth.

"You need a fence? I'm selling my fence."

Yes, he actually tried to sell me his fence. This was no halfhearted salesperson.

Still, we were nearing the end of the showroom, and he was beginning to seem worried. I had explained my stubborn dislike of busy fabric, my abhorrence of gratuitous puffiness, my disdain for Queen Anne, and we had so far come up empty.

"Wait. You'll like this one."

He pointed to a maroon recliner at the end of a row, not puffy in any way, a simple, understated pattern.

"Sit down, relax."

I did.

We left that day with a comfortable chair, with a small sofa to match, and with an order for a home entertainment cabinet—one where you could close the doors and not look at your ugly television and stereo. We didn't know we needed the cabinet and sofa until Howie told us so.

My budget for the day was $700.

Howie kept us within that budget, give or take an extra $1,800 or so.

The Secret to Being Funny

Howie *wanted* me to have a comfortable chair. Putting my middle-aged bottom in a soft, commodious seat brought him some sort of pleasure. He wasn't *just* trying to sell. He honestly thought that a comfortable chair was going to be a very good thing for me. Like all extraordinary salesmen, he truly believed.

Humor is like that. You can't force the joke. You can't pretend to be funny. You can't sit in front of your keyboard and simply decide that "I'm going to write something funny now." You have to amuse yourself and take honest pleasure in your own amusement.

I wanted to tell my story of Howie, relay his dialogue, describe his person, because frankly, I am sitting here even now grinning as I remember my time spent with him. Howie struck me as hilarious in the furniture showroom, and he still does. He was a genuine character. And I liked him.

Humor has to be honest that way. If the humor and irony of the story you tell is not fresh enough to still sneak up on you and make you smile, then don't expect it to sneak up on the reader.

Three Quick Tips

- You need a story, not just jokes. If your goal is to write compelling nonfiction, the story must always come first—what is it you are meaning to show us, and why should the reader care? It is when the humor takes a backseat to the story being told that the humorous essay is most effective and the finest writing is done.

- The humorous essay is no place to be mean or spiteful. You can probably skewer a politician or personal injury lawyer with abandon, but you should be gentle when mocking the common man. If you seem mean-spirited, if you take cheap shots, we aren't so willing to laugh.

- The funniest people don't guffaw at their own jokes or wave big "look at how funny I am" banners over their heads.

Nothing kills a joke more than the joke teller slamming a bony elbow into your ribs, winking, and shouting, "Was that funny, or what?" Subtlety is your most effective tool.

Your Humorous Essay

Are you feeling funny yet? Well then, it's time to get serious about it:

1. Think of someone who makes you laugh, not just because of what they say, but because of who they are, how they walk, the way they move their eyes, what they wear, or the way in which they eat a piece of chicken. Try to describe this person in fewer than five hundred words, through simple observation. Convince us that you actually like this person, despite the individual's comic attributes.

2. James Thurber's essays hold irony in every line. For instance, Thurber opens one of his best-known essays with, "I suppose that the high-water mark of my youth in Columbus, Ohio, was the night the bed fell on my father." The falling bed is funny, but so is the idea that this event was Thurber's "high-water mark." Columbus couldn't have been very exciting. So, what was your (comical) high-water mark?

3. Use yourself as the subject. Pick an entirely improbable thing for you to do (maybe knitting lessons, or skydiving), an improbable place for you to go (a nudist colony or Barbie Collectors Convention), or an improbable goal to set for yourself (sample every single brand and flavor of ice cream in your local grocery store over a three-month period). Go

there, do it, try it, and then write a first-person account of your experience.

4. Here is the humorist David Sedaris, writing about a time he caught a wicked virus: "It was a twenty-four-hour bug, the kind that completely empties you out and takes away your will to live. You'd get a glass of water, but that would involve standing, and so instead you just sort of stare toward the kitchen, hoping that maybe one of the pipes will burst, and the water will come to you." Is he exaggerating? Likely. But we all recognize being that ill, having no strength to even walk. What common human experience can you exaggerate slightly, so that we see the comedy within it?

5. What is the stupidest thing you have ever said?

6. Dating is inherently comical, both because so much is potentially at stake and because so many of us are so very awkward at first. What are your early (or midlife) dating memories?

7. We are often our funniest when we are at our most inept. Tell us the story of the meal you didn't manage to cook, the sink you didn't manage to repair, or the unruly child you could not tame.

8. Have you traveled overseas or into unfamiliar cultural territory? Differences in language and customs often lead to hilarious misunderstandings, like the afternoon I wandered around Madrid with a cheap Spanish phrase book asking everyone, "Do you know where I can find the room of the gentlemen?" Of course, the phrase "men's room" is not used in

Crafting the Personal Essay

Spain, so goodness knows what they thought I was asking about.

9. Do you have a dog? What has your dog seen you do that no human being has ever witnessed? Dare to tell us?

10. Not sure you've ever done anything hilariously stupid? Well, just pick up the phone and ask your older sister. She'll tell you.

A CLOSER LOOK: "PULLING TEETH"

BY DINTY W. MOORE

Any good comedian will tell you that there is no better way to kill a joke than to explain it, so it is with great trepidation that I present this brief, humorous essay of mine, along with analysis. Well, I probably shouldn't even call it humorous, because that is up to you, the reader, to decide, but I intended it to be so.

Nonetheless, just as I did with Agnes Repplier's "Leisure" and my own "Ah Wilderness!" earlier in the book, I want to present this essay in its entirety with a few insights into how the moving parts fit together and what the author intended with his various choices.

One of the choices you will note right away is that the subtitle promises "20 Reasons Why My Daughter Turning 20 Can't Come Soon Enough," and the essay itself comes in twenty numbered sections. In this way, my essay echoes the countdown format, creating what I hope is pleasant anticipation as it becomes clear the numbers are reaching an end.

Hope you enjoy.

PULLING TEETH: OR, 20 REASONS WHY MY DAUGHTER TURNING 20 CAN'T COME SOON ENOUGH BY DINTY W. MOORE

1. Here's an interesting fact: *homo erectus*, our 1.5-million-year-old evolutionary antecedent, skipped right over the teenage years, proceeding directly from cave kid to cave adult.

2. Researchers figured this out by taking cross-sections of fossilized teeth. Markings on tooth enamel, it seems, are much like tree rings. They tell us, for instance, that what modern human parents experience as an extended, oftentimes interminable period of adolescence only developed about a half million years ago.

3. Our ancestors were, in this way, like modern apes. Young apes tend to break the apron strings much earlier than humans. By the time a female chimpanzee has reached her early teen years, she can make her own nest and locate her own bananas.

4. More importantly, if a day filled with grooming her simian cousins, gnawing on twigs, and swinging from branch to branch to attract boy chimps leaves a female teen chimp feeling somehow unfulfilled, she doesn't blame anyone but herself.

5. My point? Someone should yank the teeth out of every teenage boy in my daughter's high school classroom. (I have names, and addresses, if any scientists are interested.)

6. My other point? Those same scientists should pull a few girl molars as well, and put these female teeth under a microscope. My hope here is that these molarologists will discover that some invisible change is underway. After all, if teenagers can evolve once, they can surely evolve again. Perhaps evolve beyond the prickly and entirely unnecessary adolescent stage.

THIS ESSAY, AS you can see, relies on research—in this case scientific research—to create an initial curiosity and draw in the reader. I'm not sure where I first stumbled across the fact that adolescence, as we humans know it, did not exist in early man, or for that matter in our contemporary ape cousins, but the fact stuck with me.

My own daughter, as you will learn more about soon, was deep in the midst of her own adolescence when I wrote this essay, and it just seemed funny to me to tie these two threads together—the scientific material and my own experiences. All of the facts I quote above, and below, are true, though obviously I stripped away the scientific language and put them into plain speak, then added a few banana jokes.

Clearly though, I have nearly exhausted the comic potential of the scientific matter and had better offer the reader something more soon, which I do, in section seven. I also figured the very brief sections were getting repetitive, or predictable, so you will see that I follow up here with a much longer one, and a few of varying sizes.

Finally, to quote the great actor Peter Ustinov, "Comedy is simply a funny way of being serious," and in the tradition of many of our funniest writers, I let my real emotion and concern show through beneath the fun making.

7. I have a female teenager at home. The other day, I picked up a piece of paper on my desk. *My* desk. "Don't look at that," my female teenager shouted. So I quickly returned the paper to the desk, murmured, "Sorry, didn't know it was private." She huffed. "Of course it's private." What I seemed to be looking at, in the few short moments before I was bullied into putting it back down, was a line drawing of a young woman in a dress. I think the point of the

artwork was the dress—an elaborate, original bit of *haute couture*. The design, understand, was drawn on *my* tablet, with *my* pencil. "How was I to know the drawing was private?" I asked, foolishly trying to remain in my daughter's good graces. My female teenager just glared at me, the way teenagers will glare when you have them dead to rights, when they know you're correct and they hate you for it. "Listen," she said firmly. "From now on, just assume that *everything* I do is private."

8. I am not a perfect father. Instead, I'm the "hang-in-there" type. Meaning that I have almost no idea what I am doing, but over the years I've hung in there, plugging onward, trusting that instinct— or perhaps dumb luck—will get me through. Female teenagers, of course, naturally crave a level of distance from their embarrassing, fragrant, loutish fathers, so lately I've given my daughter extra space—girls, after all, have the right to privacy. And here, then, is the rub: that space quickly begins to seem a distance, and that distance soon enough resembles a gulf. Before you know it, neither party can step across.

9. Down this road can be found any number of horrible outcomes. I know. I've imagined them all.

10. I had the good fortune to take my female teenager to Madrid last summer. Now, admittedly, Madrid in July includes surly crowds, fearsome traffic, and scorching pavement, but still, come on, this was Europe. The capital of Spain. Museums, cafes, fashion. My female teenager just moped for most of the trip, primarily because her feet hurt and she didn't take at all well to Spanish cuisine. "Why aren't you having fun?" I inquired. This is an absolutely brainless question to ask someone who seems not to be having fun, but I asked it nonetheless, more than once. "Jesus Christ," she answered. "Get over it." I persisted, stupidly imagining that I could somehow talk my daughter out of her bad humor.

"You know," I said in a calm, parental voice, "it's hard for me to have a good time when I look over and you just seem so darned miserable." She chewed on my words a moment, gave them careful consideration, then spat back, "That's your problem."

11. That *is* my problem.

12. I wish someone had taken me to Europe when I was young.

13. That's *my* problem too.

14. But I don't know what she wants, or what I'm supposed to do, or how to remain a constructive influence while being systematically frozen out of every aspect of her teenage female life. Some days, honestly, I want to scream. How do you please someone who resents your very existence? How do you stop trying? Parents, especially embarrassing male parents, *can* be a drag sometimes, but they are a biological necessity, and as much as I'd like to apologize to my female teenager for the inconvenient reality of sperm and egg and family, it is not my fault. Not really. I'm not the one who came up with it.

WELL, NOW YOU know plenty about my anxieties over fatherhood.

Why, you might ask, am I being so frank about my own shortcomings, amidst some pretty corny jokes, and why am I revealing these details of my personal life in a funny essay, instead of a more serious one?

Well, humorous essays, just like their more conventional counterparts, are based on the exploration of questions, on exploring those aspects of life that the writer wants to more fully understand. (Even stand-up comedy, often, contains just such a kernel of honest, occasionally painful, human

Crafting the Personal Essay

truth.) Humorous essayists pursue mental rabbits too, except perhaps in these essays, the mental rabbits are wearing funny straw hats and sometimes talk like Bugs Bunny.

With only six sections left to go before the magic number of 20, I decide to turn back to less personal material, specifically some information I gleaned on Charles Darwin. This allows me to circle back to the evolutionary discussion which begins my essay, and allows me to crack a joke about Darwin's fathering style. Additionally, I am able to make a serious point about finches and beaks and seed coatings, a key component of Darwin's work on the Galapagos Islands.

15. Charles Darwin had ten children, but interestingly, he didn't take any of them along to the islands.

16. So I'm back to the teeth. Maybe, just maybe, evolution is occurring even now, and maybe female teenagers are developing beyond this tendency toward prickly unreasonableness. Perhaps this whole problem is just a half-million year aberration, a necessary but ridiculous step along the evolutionary continuum.

17. Or possibly, like those Galapagos finches Darwin was so fond of, parents themselves will adapt new beaks, allowing them to break open this tougher seed coating.

18. As for my daughter, she will stop being a teenager eventually. She will turn twenty. I've heard that can happen.

19. For now though, just getting my female teenager to speak to me is like … well … like pulling teeth.

20. And I don't like pulling teeth. It tends to be painful on both ends.

WRITE WHAT YOU WISH YOU KNEW

"We have to continually be jumping off cliffs and developing our wings on the way down."
—Kurt Vonnegut

There are plenty of folks who consider coffee to be the most critical fuel for good writing, and while I don't by any means want to speak poorly of coffee, which has pulled me through countless deadlines, I must differ with those folks and suggest that fresh, unexpected information is a far better source of authorial energy.

Nothing opens the minds, lifts us out of a rut, or suggests innovative directions for story or thought than finding a bright new fact, living a novel experience, or seeing something we've never seen before.

Whoever first said "Write what you know" had it all wrong, I'm afraid. "Do your research" is a far better morsel of advice.

Research, though, need not be the same as homework—it doesn't have to be tedious. Research can include jumping in your car and driving to the Uruguayan restaurant on the far side of town to taste your first *chivito*, taking ten minutes to talk with the man who repairs your gas furnace—does he lose sleep worrying about a mistake, given that what he fixes day in, day out is in some ways similar to a giant bomb placed in people's basements?—or arranging to take a kayak trip down a gentle river when you've never done so before. Research can be as simple as running to the library or a search engine to find the precise name of something, instead of making a general guess, or it can be a learning project that takes years and develops as you go.

No matter how you do it, research and learning enhance and improve your essays in countless ways.

If you don't believe me, listen to essayist Philip Lopate muse on where to start one's writing:

"... what do we need to generate nonfiction? I would say, curiosity. It sounds more tepid than obsession, but it's a lot more dependable in the long run. You follow out a strand of curiosity and pretty soon you've got an interesting digression, a whole chapter, a book proposal, a book."

 WRITING EXERCISE: GETTING OUT OF THE CHAIR

How do you harness your curiosity?

Well, imagine that you weren't sitting in your chair reading this book right now, and that you didn't have firm plans to get up tomorrow morning to sit in front of your keyboard, and that you didn't have a job or family responsibilities, and that you simply had all the free time in the world.

Imagine that, and then fill in some of the blanks that follow:

I've always wanted to _____

I'd be afraid to _____

I never seem to have the time to _____

When I was a child I loved to _____, but now I haven't done it for years.

When I was a child, I really wanted to _____ when I grew up.

I think _____ must be a fascinating hobby.

I think _____ must be a very interesting way to earn a living.

I think _____ must be a very strange way to earn a living.

I think _____ must be a very anxiety-ridden way to earn a living.

I think _____ is probably the most interesting corner in my city or town.

I've always meant to ask _____ about her job.

I have always meant to ask _____ about her hobby.

I wonder what _____ tastes like.

I wonder what _____ smells like.

I wonder what _____ feels like.

How does someone become qualified to

_____

When I watch television/sports/ballet, I often wonder how someone ends up with a job such as _____

I have no idea how _____ is made.

I eat _____ every day yet I don't really know where it comes from.

I sure would like to see a _____

INVESTIGATING THE FOREIGN

My first two books were both nonfiction explorations of "foreign" cultures, or cultures that were foreign to me at least, yet I never left the country to write these books and never got on an airplane. I did a lot of reading of course, and for my in-person research, I jumped into my little Ford economy car and drove six-hours this way, ten hours that way, or sometimes just fifteen minutes up the road. Most of this was done on weekends. I had a job that kept me busy, a family, and all of the usual pulls on my time, so I couldn't drop everything and disappear for a year.

What cultures am I talking about?

My first book, *The Emperor's Virtual Clothes*, was an attempt to understand the Internet, and the people who were using it for gaming, socializing, political action, artistic promotion, therapy, small business, and so on. This nonfiction project began in 1994, when very few people had access to the Internet and e-mail was still something new and unfamiliar. CNN and NBC and *The Wall Street Journal* were all predicting that this "amazing new thing" was going to change everything about our lives, but none of these news outlets seemed able to say just exactly how our lives might change. I was curious to find out, so I tracked down those early adopters who were already chindeep in pixels and asked the question, "How has it changed them?"

My second book, *The Accidental Buddhist,* began much the same way. I noticed numerous magazine features about people in America—inner-city police officers, school teachers, kids with test anxiety, stressed office workers—turning to the basic teachings of Buddhism and mindfulness to cope with the pressures of their lives. I became curious as to how Buddhism, a 2,500-year-old philosophy, rooted firmly in Asian culture, could ever really fit into the go-go, faster-faster pace of late twentieth-century American culture, and whether the folks who were adapting Buddhism were serious or just pretending. So I went on weekend Buddhist retreats, five-day silent Zen *sesshins,* met with teachers and students, and the folks who make those rounded *zafu* pillows used for meditation, and tried it all for myself.

What was remarkable, fortuitous, and ultimately a great gift, is that the more I learned about these "foreign" cultures, the more curious I became, and before long these two books began to write themselves. I was full of questions, and each chapter became one of the answers along the way.

So yes, I'm a little gung ho on writing out of curiosity rather than knowledge. If you haven't done enough of this in your own writing, I heartily recommend you give it a try.

Here are four authors who also write what they don't know—or perhaps put more accurately, write what they didn't know when they started—and the strategies they used to create compelling nonfiction:

First, You Must Observe

Susan Orlean is best known for her quirky *New Yorker* profiles and features, but one aspect of her writing that always interests me is the close observation and description she brings to the page. Give Orlean a subject about which she knows nothing and soon enough she will see it with more clarity than anyone else in the room.

Susan Orlean doesn't accomplish this, of course, by merely glancing at her subjects and learning a few simple facts. She studies her subjects, and studies them closely, over time.

For instance, here is a short bit from her profile of Biff, a show dog:

> If you're ever around Biff while you're eating something he wants to taste—cold roast beef, a Wheatables cracker, chocolate, pasta, aspirin, whatever—he will stare at you across the pleated bridge of his nose and let his eyes sag and his lips tremble and allow a little bead of drool to percolate at the edge of his mouth until you feel so crummy that you give him some.

That's funny, but also—if you've ever really paid attention to a begging dog—spot on accurate.

Orleans applies the same intense scrutiny to every subject she encounters, including John Laroche, a rare plants dealer who eventually became the central character in her book *The Orchid Thief*. Orlean thought she was simply off on another brief magazine assignment, but she let what she didn't know capture her mind.

"I never imagined that I would end up spending ... two years shadowing Laroche and exploring the odd, passionate world of orchid fanatics," she has written of her resultant book project. "I certainly never imagined that I would willingly hike through the swamps of South Florida—but that's what writing a book does to you."

The Orchid Thief, along with becoming a best seller, was adapted to become the movie *Adaptation,* in which Orlean herself was played by Meryl Streep.

Now that's payback for taking some chances. We should all find ourselves wandering unexpectedly though our own mucky Florida swamps.

Learn the Facts, but Always Remember the People

Susan Orlean planned to investigate rare plants and smuggling but ended up finding the orchid dealer every bit as compelling as her intended subject. That's not really so great a surprise if you know Orlean's work.

Asked to write about tattoo parlors becoming legal again in Massachusetts after a nearly four-decade ban, she started this way:

> Stephan Lanphear ... is rangy and regular-looking, with choppy brown hair and a long, sweet face— the sort of young guy you might sit next to on a bus and not remember later. Naked, he would be easier to keep in mind, because he is intricately marked, wrist to neck to waist to ankle, working his way into what tattoo artists call a full body suit.

Many writers might have approached that subject by focusing on the legal fight that led to scrapping the Massachusetts tattoo prohibition, or by explaining the intricacies of the law, or quoting statistics on how much is spent in a tattoo parlor and what it does to the state's tax base.

But you and I know what we find interesting, and it is usually not statistics or the intricacies of the law. We find people interesting, in all of their splendid difference and glory.

The people *are* the story.

Find the Subject Within the Subject

Mark Twain, the novelist best known for his characters Tom Sawyer and Huckleberry Finn, began his writing career as a journalist and essayist, often writing letters back to his hometown paper based on his exotic travels.

Not surprisingly, given his lifelong interest in the Mississippi River region, one of his essayistic outings focused on New Orleans, specifically on the above-ground cemeteries (necessary because if you dig just a few inches down in below-sea-level New Orleans, you quickly hit the water table).

Here is Twain, from his essay "Hygiene and Sentiment":

> They bury their dead in vaults, above the ground. These vaults have a resemblance to houses— sometimes to temples; are built of marble, generally; are architecturally graceful and shapely; they face the walks and driveways of the cemetery: and when one moves through the midst of a thousand or so of them and sees their white roofs and gables stretching into the distance on every hand, the phrase "city of the dead" has all at once a meaning to him. Many of the cemeteries are beautiful, and are kept in perfect order. When one goes from the levee or the business streets near it, to a cemetery, he observes to himself that if those people down there would live as neatly while they are alive as they do after they are dead, they would find many advantages in it; and besides, their quarter would be the wonder and admiration of the business world.

Twain has injected his usual wry sarcasm here, expressing the wish that people maintained their homes as well as they do the graves of their relatives, but eventually he cues the reader into his deeper subject, what really interests him about graves:

> It is all grotesque, ghastly, horrible. Graveyards may have been justifiable in the bygone ages, when nobody knew that for every dead body put into the ground, to glut the earth and the plant-roots and the air with disease-germs, five or fifty, or maybe a hundred, persons must die before their proper time; but they are hardly justifiable now...

Twain backs up his claim that graveyards open us all to the risks of infectious disease (or at least, that they did a century or so ago) by citing the studies of a physician and scientist, then moves his subject further along to what bothers him even more than matters of hygiene.

Burial, he asserts, is a simple waste of money. "One and one-fourth times more money is expended annually in funerals in the United States," he writes, "than the Government expends for public-school purposes."

A few more statistics follow, citing what he sees as a wasted expense, until he remembers that the story is almost always best told through the people themselves, and closes his essay by telling the tale of an acquaintance, a man who earns his living doing odd jobs:

> He never earns above four hundred dollars in a year, and as he has a wife and several young children, the closest scrimping is necessary to get him through to the end of the twelve months debtless. To such a man a funeral is a colossal financial

Crafting the Personal Essay

disaster. While I was writing one of the preceding chapters, this man lost a little child. He walked the town over with a friend, trying to find a coffin that was within his means. He bought the very cheapest one he could find, plain wood, stained. It cost him twenty-six dollars. It would have cost less than four, probably, if it had been built to put something useful into. He and his family will feel that outlay a good many months.

Obsession Is Not Just a Perfume

Philip Lopate, the essayist who reminded us near the beginning of this chapter that "curiosity ... sounds more tepid than obsession, but it's a lot more dependable in the long run," wrote a book a few years back that entailed walking the entire circumference of Manhattan, attempting to access the waterfront. Manhattan, remember, is an island, surrounded by water on all sides, but for the most part the rivers are hard to reach, and Lopate had to struggle to get to water's edge.

That project certainly sounds obsessive to me, but Lopate has confessed that he was not so much fanatical about the inaccessible waterfront as he was looking for an interesting idea for a book. He was, in other words, faking it just a bit.

Remember the discussion of persona in chapter twelve? To briefly remind you, we discussed that honest writers of nonfiction don't invent a personality or pretend to be someone we are not, but we do sometimes polish up a side of ourselves and present it to the reader with heightened energy.

Why? Because a committed voice in writing, someone who knows what they are seeking and who is confident of their questions is more pleasurable to follow on the page than someone who seems unsure of what they are doing, why they are doing it, or why the reader should care. Henry David Thoreau truly wanted to know what it would mean to live more simply, but historians and literary scholars will tell you that he took that interest and exaggerated just a bit.

Some decades back, the author George Plimpton made a name for himself by taking on certain unusual experiences, such as practicing with the Detroit Lions football team and sparring with light-heavyweight champ Archie Moore.

More recently, author A. J. Jacobs paid homage to Plimpton's "immersion" strategy with two new books, *The Know-It-All: One Man's Humble Quest to Become the Smartest Person in the World,* wherein Jacobs read the entire Encyclopedia Britannica, cover to cover, and *The Year of Living Biblically: One Man's Humble Quest to Follow the Bible as Literally as Possible,* a title that pretty much explains itself.

Is Jacobs obsessed, clever, gimmicky, or something else entirely? I'll let you decide, but he seems never at a loss for ideas, and his readers have fun following his goofy self-made adventures.

"I feel lucky about being able to make a living this way," Jacobs has said. "It's like going to school your whole life, getting crash courses on these really interesting topics."

Well, you can do that too.

 ## WRITING EXERCISE: WHAT IF YOU SPENT ONE WEEK?

Perhaps you aren't quite ready to tackle an obsessive book project like Jacobs did in *The Year of Living*

Crafting the Personal Essay

Biblically, but the same approach can also work in the essay-length writing project.

Essayist Robin Hemley was obsessed with just how lousy his experience in summer camp had been when he was a mere boy, so at age forty-something he went back, stayed in a cabin with the kids, drank bug juice, took craft class, and tried to do the experience over. What resulted was a pretty funny essay.

What could you do?

Return to your first job ever—packing groceries, flipping burgers, delivering newspapers—to see what has changed?

Spend a week at a silent spiritual retreat or take yoga twice a day and eat nothing but raw foods?

What if you spent seven days volunteering in a soup kitchen (which would be a good thing on its own, of course), or a week cleaning up the litter in a dilapidated neighborhood on the other side of town, talking to folks as you went along?

How about a week doing nothing but watching The Food Network, every waking minute? How hungry would you become? Or would you quickly grow tired of food?

Spend a week trying not to answer the question "How are you doing?" with a mindless, "Just fine!" Instead, stop and talk with the person who asks the question, and then find how they are doing, *really*. What would you learn, about yourself and others?

Bake cookies for every family up and down your street, ring the doorbell and deliver them, for no good reason at all. I hope all of your reactions would be positive, but write about them either way.

The list could go on and on.

Spend five minutes right now making your own list. Don't censor yourself by thinking "that would be too hard" or "too weird," just write down every single goofy or serious, noble or frivolous idea you can come up with. You don't have to follow through on the idea, so let your imagination wander.

Keep that list. It may just lead somewhere interesting.

MY ASSAY: WHEREIN THE AUTHOR ATTEMPTS TO FOLLOW HIS OWN ADVICE

In truth, my entire essay, now titled "Of Idle People Who Rove About," involves the impulse to write based on what I do not know.

I didn't know anything about Boca Raton before I arrived, so I wandered as many parts of the city as I could. I didn't know how to get to the ocean as a mere pedestrian with no VIP access, so I improvised and found a way. I didn't see anyone walking along the I-95 overpass and wasn't sure if it could be successfully traversed, so I tried. When the kind graduate student offered me the easy way out—"I could pick you up every day before class," she said—I politely declined. I trusted my instinct that trying something new would be the better option, and it was.

I'm not staking any claim to being a great adventurer—I'll leave that honor to Marco Polo, Ernest Shackleton, or Lewis and Clark—but my curiosity has always served me well as a writer, along with my willingness to hop into a canoe or ask a stranger an unusual question.

I highly recommend you work to cultivate your own inquisitive side.

NEED SOME FREE TIME?

Do you still believe that old axiom, "Write what you know"?

Okay, but poet Howard Nemerov has some advice for you: "Write what you know. That should leave you with a lot of free time."

17

WRITING THE NATURE ESSAY

*"The clearest way into the Universe is through
a forest wilderness."*
—John Muir

The personal essay is keenly suited to an appreciation of nature, if for no other reason than that the essay's meandering disposition so often resembles a morning's stroll through the forest or an afternoon spent kayaking a sun-dappled lake. Walking can be like thinking, and the gentle path of the essay can easily resemble those ambling thought patterns as well.

Nature-loving writers have known this all along, or discovered it anew. Listen to early nineteenth-century British essayist William Hazlitt, for instance, in his essay "On Going a Journey":

> One of the pleasantest things in the world is going a journey; but I like to go by myself ... When I am in the country I wish to vegetate like the country. I am not for criticizing hedge-rows and black cattle. I go out of town in order to forget the town and all that is in it. ... The soul of a journey is liberty, perfect liberty, to think, feel, do, just as one pleases.

There are, in fact, countless examples of essayists, both classic and contemporary, who take nature as their subject. If you are lucky enough to have read widely in the essay, you are no doubt thinking of Henry David Thoreau right now or perhaps more-recent writers such as Annie Dillard or Terry Tempest Williams.

Important to remember, however, is that the path to exceptional nature writing does not end with abstractly *appreciating* nature or just waxing philosophically about a glorious sunrise. The reader is glad to know that you are thankful for nature's beauty and diversity, certainly, but what readers really seek in a superior nature essay is for the writer to show us something new or something fairly common but in a new way. We want to see the world around us—birds, fish, trees, clouds, plants, mud—as we have not seen them before, and good nature writing allows us that privilege and pleasure.

To do this, you as writer must observe very closely, and with not just a patient eye but an informed eye. This takes some time, demanding that you become intimately associated with your local forest, your favorite lakeshore, or the small but still diverse wetland tucked away in the back of your housing development. But it is well worth the effort.

A Note on Seasoning

Thoreau, of course, structured his classic book around a year spent at Walden Pond, and that year allowed him to chronicle not just what he saw, but how it changed through the seasons. That is one of the more-intriguing characteristics of nature, of course: The way it is always coming and going, drifting away and then returning once more.

Consider this excerpt from his journal:

> This is June, the month of grass and leaves ... Already the Aspens are trembling again, and a new summer is offered me. I feel a little fluttered in my thoughts, as if I might be too late. Each season is but an infinitesimal point. It no sooner comes than it is gone ...

Or consider Marcia Bonta, author of nine books and more than three hundred magazine articles, many of them based on the forest-covered, mountaintop farm in Central Pennsylvania where she and her husband raised three sons. Four of Bonta's best-known volumes, *Appalachian Spring, Appalachian Summer, Appalachian Autumn,* and *Appalachian Winter,* offer day-by-day accounts of her hikes through the isolated roads and trails of her 500-acre farm, noting the minute transformations of the season as well as the more dramatic ones (bears, migratory eagles, intrusive clear-cutting on a neighbors property).

Listen to this excerpt from her prologue to the book:

> Sometime in early August, summer's humidity is blown away for a day or two. Intimations of autumn are in the air. Billowing clouds, pushed along by the cleansing winds, race across the blue sky. The breast-high grasses of First Field seethe and ripple like a restless ocean. Eagerly I scan the sky for migrating raptors, and instead I spot a turkey vulture sporting in the wind, dipping back and forth, up and down, as if for the sheer joy of it.

Nature is about change, interaction, and rejuvenation. Return to that same little bend in the creek every three days as winter turns to spring, and then write.

Three Quick Tips

- Learn to identify trees, grasses, insects, leaves, rodents, birds, by using widely available guidebooks, either through the library or your local bookstore. A sentence that begins "there is a scarlet tanager on the red blaze maple ..." is so much more interesting than "a bird lands on a nearby tree."

- The key to successful nature writing often comes *before* you put pen to paper; it comes in the ability to see what is not commonly seen. Though we can all agree that a rainy summer day can be cleansing to the soul and that baby animals of almost any sort are cute as can be, a piece of writing that merely reminds us of these obvious points has nothing to say. The nature essayist finds the unexpected angle and is then meticulously attentive until something unforeseen is discovered.

- You can't write about nature without getting your hands and trousers a little dirty. But that's part of the fun.

Your Nature Essay

The highest-quality nature writing is cognizant of what scientists have discovered, and concerned with whatever other knowledge naturalists and similar experts have accumulated over the centuries, but the focus should always return to the *personal* observations of the writer. You are not writing just about birds and trees, seashores and forests, foxes and poison sumac; you are writing about how you respond to these things, how they affect your life, and what pleases or astonishes you.

Without your personal, distinctive voice, there is no reason for the essay.

So remember that, always, as you follow these varied prompts.

1. Annie Dillard, in her essay "Living Like Weasels," tells us, "I have been thinking about weasels because I saw one last week. I startled a weasel who startled me, and we exchanged a long glance." That locking of eyes serves as an occasion for Dillard to consider the difference between her protected life and life in the predatory wilderness, and also what she might learn from this secretive creature. What can you learn from the mammals, birds, or even plants that you observe closely? What do they know that we as humans may have forgotten?

2. Take some twigs and some string and a ruler and mark off one-square-foot of forest floor, or of beach sand, or of stream bank. Now look at the surface, dig beneath the surface, sit silently and see what crawls out, about, or over the square-foot you've chosen. Consider the textures, the colors, and the density of the soil. Examine everything there, and then write for five minutes about that square foot of territory. (HINT: This often works best when you choose a transitional area: where the edge of the wooded land bleeds into open meadow, or where sea grass meets open sand.)

3. Don't overlook your own garden.

4. Yet remember this: While it may be easy to write one thousand words about your vegetable garden, writing one thousand words about just one tomato

Crafting the Personal Essay

plant in your garden forces you to get beyond the usual observations and find something fresh to say.

5. There is nature, of course, even in an urban setting. Weeds flourish in the openings found between cracked sidewalk sections. Pigeons roost in odd corners of empty buildings. Nature is not always beautiful and pristine. Even the rough spots are interesting.

6. I am fascinated by birds. The more I watch them, the more I notice how different the flight patterns and landing patterns and flocking behaviors are for each species, and when I really watch and study, I begin to understand that these patterns are almost always dictated by the availability of different foods (except when mating comes into play, of course). Pick a blue jay, a robin, and a yellow finch (or any three birds native to your area) and notice not just what is common to the birds, but what makes each of them so different.

7. Instead of writing about a tree, write about the bark.

8. Instead of writing about a flower, focus on the seeds.

9. Bugs are fascinating. Even the scary ones.

10. Keep a journal. Note changes.

11. An essay of any sort can include what you *don't* understand, and that's true here too.

12. Try to see from the animal's point-of-view. If you live in a portion of suburbia that is grappling with an escalating deer population, an area where homeowners are (rightly) worried about decimated

shrubbery, devastated gardens, and possible roadway collisions, explore the problem from the other side. What are the deer worried about?

13. Fresh spring buds and greenery can be so wonderfully revitalizing, but remember that death and decay are also an important part of nature's cycle. The forest floor is one enormous compost pile, recycling nutrients into the soil for next year's growth. We humans, however, often remove every sign of dead leaf or cut grass from our lawns, only to then buy gigantic bags of chemical fertilizer to spread in spring and fall. Don't rant, or judge, but thoughtfully consider how we arrived at this ironic moment in man's relationship to the land around him.

14. Long-abandoned farmland is fascinating to explore.

15. If you can afford to travel to the South Pole, by all means do so (and take me with you), but remember that you can also learn about nature and find a subject for your writing by simply planting one seed in a tiny pot by the window on the desk where you sit and scribbling each morning.

WRITING THE
TRAVEL ESSAY

*"Travel and change of place impart new vigor
to the mind."*

—Seneca

One of the finest and most-satisfying adventures of my life so far was the time I canoed through whitewater rapids down the lower canyons of the Rio Grande River, just east of Big Bend National Park in southern Texas. You read about this trip in an earlier chapter, when we took a closer look at the essay "Ah, Wilderness! Humans, Hawks, and Environmental Correctness on the Muddy Rio Grande."

Each day of that trip brought new sights and new adventures—as might be expected of such a grand landscape and precarious mode of travel—and it was in my attempt to put this river journey into words that I discovered what every other travel writer has probably discovered as well:

- Travel writing is easy, because travel has a natural story arc. We enter the canyon, we are surrounded by high canyon walls for days and days, facing fresh obstacles with each passing mile, and eventually we come out the other side. Think how many novels, short stories, and memoirs mimic that very structure. Have you heard of Homer's epic poem *The Odyssey,* for instance? Even if you are not on an "adventure" trip, you still have a natural beginning in your arrival, a natural middle with your stay, and a natural ending around your departure. Time and again, the journey structure seems to work.

- Travel writing is very, very hard. As writers, we usually come to understand our topics and our feelings toward them over the course of years, not days. We understand the culture we live in by growing up within that culture. We understand family love and family woes by being members of a family for decades. We write about our spiritual journeys after years of searching and seeking. By definition, however, a travel writer is often just passing through. The result is that a travel writer runs the risk of noticing only the slick, shallow surface of things, not the truth that lies beneath.

While I remain grateful for that aspect of travel that makes the writing easy, I still have not found the precise antidote for what makes it so difficult, except to be aware of the dangers of shallow observation and to try very diligently to avoid them.

A Reminder to Avoid Quaint Sentimentality

Though I understand where the notion comes from, I must admit my frustration with travel essays that reveal little more than "I went to this exotic location and boy was it ever different!"

Well, of course it was different!

Foreign lands *are* different, the food *is* unusual (to you), and the unfamiliar customs are sometimes charming. Though there remains something exhilarating about discovering these delightful differences firsthand, there is nothing new in the discovery.

So, just as you should avoid being the ignorant visitor, the one who insists that foreign lands should be "just like home," with all of the familiar comforts and menu items, avoid as well the tendency to over-romanticize. The indigenous woman selling handcrafted souvenirs in the village square is charming and evocative maybe, but she is also a person, with children and grandchildren, perhaps a stack of debt and worries back home, and maybe even some arthritis in her knees. Don't make the mistake of assuming her life is simple, easier, or less stressful than your own.

When travelling, try to see what is really there, not what past travel articles—many of them riddled with clichés—tell you will be there.

Three Quick Tips

• Read as much as you can about your destination before you arrive, and don't just read the guidebooks. Read up on the region's history and economy, explore the cooking and agriculture, and try to understand religious observances. This way, if you see something unfamiliar or peculiar, you'll have a better chance of understanding the reasoning behind the custom.

• Newspaper travel sections often reduce travel writing to a list of hotels and tourist-friendly restaurants. These articles can be useful, certainly, to first-time travelers, but as an essayist, remember that you are digging for deeper treasure, looking for meaning in an experience, not just bargains.

- There is a difference between a travel writer and a tourist. A tourist is on vacation; a travel writer is on a pursuit.

Your Travel Essay

Try some of the following prompts to get your travel essay wheels turning:

1. You needn't go overseas. If you live in the city, go to the country and attend an antique farm equipment auction or learn to make goat cheese. If you live in the country, spend a long weekend in Chicago or New York City.

2. But if you do the latter, don't try to "cover" the whole city in three days. All you will have then is a list of destinations. Instead, pick an obscure neighborhood, eight square blocks, and really get to know the area up close.

3. Add people to your story. If you speak the language of the area you are visiting, that's a great advantage, but if you do not, find someone local who speaks English. Buy them coffee or lunch and ask them questions. Most people are flattered and eager to talk about the place where they live.

4. Travel writer Pico Iyer, author of *The Global Soul: Jet Lag, Shopping Malls, and the Search for Home*, advises skipping the normal attractions. He seeks out the "... new, absolutely contemporary,

and constantly shifting wonders of the modern world." For example, in his often-anthologized essays, Iyer chronicles airport culture instead of cathedrals and explores the world's largest Kentucky Fried Chicken, found just off Tiananmen Square, near the Mao Tse-tung mausoleum. In other words, don't try to capture what you can see on every tourist postcard. If it is on the postcards, it is already a cliché.

5. Not all travel is uplifting and life-affirming. Were you pick-pocketed? Write about it. Do you suspect the cabdrivers of inflating their prices? Well, write about that and how it makes you feel.

6. Fly to Paris, Berlin, Mexico City, or Minneapolis. After a good lunch and a revitalizing nap, take out a map of the area—maybe large enough to cover a 50-mile-radius. Now close your eyes and point. Find a way to get to wherever your finger landed, write about how you got there and the surprises along the way.

7. When you find yourself in a location where the cuisine seems very exotic, seek out cooking classes. Or offer the cook in your hotel a small tip to at least let you observe.

8. In lieu of the grand, "written-about-two-thousand-times-each-year" medieval cathedral, seek out the small place of worship that no one visits except the people who actually live and pray there.

9. Bring your*self* into the travel, and the travel essay. If you are a sixty-year-old, recently widowed

woman who spent her life farming and raising dairy cows, your response to the French countryside should reflect that, and thus be very different from a response written by a twenty-five-year-old elementary school teacher.

10. Be enthusiastic and curious. It will make your travel more interesting and will always show through in the writing.

writing the personal essay is like chasing mental rabbits

PART TWO
REACHING
READERS

ON A REGULAR
WRITING ROUTINE

*"All the good writing I've done in the last ten years
has been done in the first twenty minutes after the
first time I wanted to leave the room."*
—Ron Carlson

Sometimes writing seems to be the most complicated, vexing, mysterious enterprise imaginable, but at other times I need only take a step back, reconsider, and some of it seems quite straightforward.

For instance, here is one of the simple parts:

Those men and women who sit down with pen in hand, or computer keyboard on the desk, and stay there, regularly, no matter how stuck or uninteresting they feel on a given day, end up creating new essays, poems, or stories, and eventually find readers and enjoy the rewards of getting published. Those, however, who wait for inspiration to strike, for retirement, or for the new drapes to arrive in order to make their home writing office "just perfect," end up dreaming about and talking about writing, but usually produce very little.

This advice is nothing new, of course. Countless writers have suggested over the years that the hardest, and most crucial, part of the enterprise is attaching the seat of the pants to the seat of the chair and applying oneself consistently to the task of moving words around on the page.

Even Flannery O'Connor, the acclaimed novelist and short story writer, attributes her enormous success to sheer diligence rather than brilliance:

> I'm a full-time believer in writing habits, pedestrian as it all may sound. You may be able to do without them if you have genius but most of us only have talent and this is simply something that has to be assisted all the time by physical and mental habits or it dries up and blows away.

O'Connor explains, in her excellent book *The Habit of Being*, that she writes two hours a day, "because that's all the energy I have." She suffered from severe lupus, so many of her daily tasks were difficult, but O'Connor treated writing like a job, something that had to be done, no matter how good or bad, inspired or uninspired she felt.

Most successful writers share that attitude, putting in the time even if they feel devoid of ideas, sentence clumsy, or just plain discouraged.

How Much Time?

I've known a few writers who manage eight hours a day, just as if they were pulling a shift at the "writing" factory, but that's unusual. Most writers I've spoken with over the years manage two to four hours, and maybe a few more when really focused on finishing a project.

But here's the simple truth: Many writers—perhaps you included—don't have four to eight hours every day to devote to writing. We may wish that we had that sort of time to devote to our passion, but we have "other" jobs and family and groceries and laundry and life in general. But don't let that become an excuse for not even trying. Even thirty minutes, twice a week, is going to make you a better writer. Just thirty minutes. But *you have to show up*, as if you had a boss who was regularly studying your time card, and as if you wouldn't get paid otherwise.

The boss studying your time card is *you*, of course, and the pay envelope comes filled with fresh material, new confidence, and strengthened writing skills.

Good Days and Bad Days

The benefits of keeping a regular writing routine sound good, don't they?

Let me be honest: It works.

Now let me be totally honest: not all of the time.

As a writer, you are going to have bad days, or stretches of bad days, where nothing that you write seems good enough. You are going to have days where your brain rests limply in your skull emitting all of the vibrancy and intelligence of a damp and moldy sponge. You are going to have days where even forming a complete sentence on the page seems far out of your grasp.

Even the best, most seasoned writers have those days.

Consider another quote from Flannery O'Connor, explaining why you need to be present and prepared for the work of writing, no matter what:

> Sometimes I work for months and have to throw everything away, but I don't think any of that was time wasted. Something goes on that makes it easier when it does come well. And the fact is

Crafting the Personal Essay

> if you don't sit there every day, the day it would
> come well, you won't be sitting there.

Or, in other words, those bad days are going to come one way or another. That's simply a fact of the writing life. Thus, sitting in your chair, struggling through the gobbledygook that comes out of your brain, on one of those bad days, is still a productive effort, because you are getting one of your inevitable bad days out of the way.

Moreover, if you use the bad days as an excuse not to be in your chair, you might miss one of the good days, *because you can't predict when they might come.*

I've had weeks where I accomplished five days work in one day, after four days of hemming and hawing and pushing my pencil back and forth.

Writing is a mysterious process.

All you can do is open yourself to the possibilities, be willing to work, and get at it.

Feedback and Writing Groups

One good way to encourage yourself in a regular routine of writing is to have someone waiting on the other end to see what you have written. Deadlines make wonderful motivational tools.

One tried-and-true method of establishing deadlines is to form a writing group—that could mean a group of two or a group of eight or anywhere in between—that meets on a regular schedule. So, for instance, if you and three local writers meet every third Thursday at 7 P.M., some of you (or all of you, depending on your group size) will have committed to bring copies of your rough drafts for discussion. The simple human urge not to show up empty-handed when others are expecting an essay, poem, story, or chapter has pushed countless writers to finish work that might otherwise have been pushed aside by chores, work, and fatigue. Plus, you have readers, and having someone read and care about your work is highly gratifying.

Allow me to give just a little bit of advice on writing groups, however.

Ten Tips for Writing Groups

1. The best writing groups achieve a delicate balance between supportive and challenging. You want friendly folks who will be gentle and encouraging, but at the same time the best groups push everyone within the group to improve their writing week to week. Writers, like athletes, are always trying to improve their last performance.

2. The balance discussed above is hard to reach, so be patient. If a member of your group is consistently rude, negative, or dismissive, however, it may be time to reconstitute the group. On the same token, if a member always says "Oh, this is so good, don't change a word of it," demand more. Ask *everyone* to address both what is good and what can be improved.

3. Though we often refer to what we bring to our writing groups as "rough drafts," don't confuse this with *first* drafts. If you bring in a first draft and the group tells you that this rough, early effort at your subject seems incomplete and unfocused, but has great potential, you are wasting your own time and the time of others in your group, because you

already knew that: All early drafts are incomplete, lack focus, and have potential.

4. The best work to share with other writers is an essay that you have been struggling with for a while, an essay that you feel has come together into some beginning firmness of purpose and voice, but an essay that is still vexing you, not quite done.

5. Often, in a group of this sort, you can learn more about writing when the group is considering the work of someone *other than you*. When your own poem, essay, or story is "up for workshop," it is easy (and normal) to just listen for the thumbs up or thumbs down and hope for more ups than downs. But when the group is considering the work of Carol, the schoolteacher across the table from you, it is time to strap on your listening and thinking caps.

6. Questions to ask yourself while the group is considering the work of Carol, the schoolteacher across the table: *What really worked in Carol's writing, and how can I learn to do this just as well? What didn't work in Carol's essay, and am I guilty of the same sloppiness, self-indulgence, over-explanation, vagueness, or lack of description in my own work? If Carol's essay were my essay, what would I do differently? What's the most vibrant paragraph in this essay and what makes it so alive on the page?*

7. When the group is discussing your work, listen to every bit of opinion and feedback. (Better yet, jot down notes.) But also heed this advice from best-selling science fiction and fantasy author

Neil Gaiman: "Remember: when people tell you something's wrong or doesn't work for them, they are almost always right. When they tell you exactly what they think is wrong and how to fix it, they are almost always wrong."

8. The best writing groups stay focused for the full hour or two hours, or whatever time has been allotted, to discussing writing and improvement. Politely rein in group members who try to turn every meeting into a chat about children and dogs. That can come later.

9. One way to keep the atmosphere serious is to find somewhere to meet other than someone's home, since home life (and the nearby kitchen) offer endless distractions. Often bookstores and libraries are willing to give space to writing groups.

10. It is good to have a leader, someone who can say, "We seem to be repeating the same advice, let's move on," or "Let Sam talk next—he hasn't had his chance." In informal groups, it often works to just rotate leadership every time you meet so that everyone feels part of the group and no one person comes to dominate.

Just about everything I say in my ten tips above applies to formal writing workshops as well, at your local college or writing center, though in those instances you have a designated leader, and he or she has responsibility for keeping the group on task.

If you can't find a group, or a class, it also works to just recruit a good friend (one who likes and reads books regularly), and promise that friend, "I will have a new draft of my story to show you when we meet for coffee next Saturday." That's a deadline. Tell your friend the following: "I want gentle honesty. Tell me what you like, but be straightforward too about what is not clear, or where I tend to ramble." Praise is good, but even better are helpful suggestions that allow you to make a piece of writing twice as wonderful.

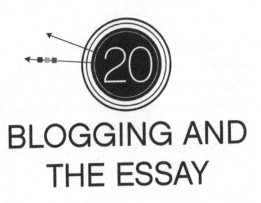

BLOGGING AND THE ESSAY

"The point of the essay is to change things."
—Edward Tufte

Let me remind you of the definition of *essay* I shared with you near the beginning of this book:

> The personal essay is a gentle art, an idiosyncratic combination of the author's discrete sensibilities and the endless possibilities of meaning and connection. The essay is graceful, wise, and always surprising. The essay invites extreme playfulness and almost endless flexibility.

Combine discrete sensibilities with endless possibilities of meaning and connection and extremes of playfulness and flexibility, and you are pretty accurately describing what some of the best bloggers do. Whether blogging about food, politics, parenthood, or how to raise puppies, the blogger is always trying out new ideas, looking for connections, and offering his or her discrete sensibility on the subject.

Why blog?

Blogging is free, and good practice. If you promise those who read your blog that you will update three times a week, then you've given yourself a deadline. Though an audience is not guaranteed, it is certainly easier to find an audience online compared to leaving what you write on the hard drive of your computer (where only hackers and technicians will ever stumble upon it).

The Atlantic (magazine) blogger Andrew Sullivan has also noted the similarity between contemporary Web logs and the essay tradition. "Montaigne was living his skepticism, daring to show how a writer evolves," he writes, adding that to blog is "to let go of your writing in a way, to hold it at arm's length, open it to scrutiny, allow it to float in the ether for a while, and to let others, as Montaigne did, pivot you toward relative truth."

In other words, a blog can be a discussion of sorts, a place for consideration, just like the classical essay form back in history.

Five Tips for Bloggers

1. The simplest and easiest online platforms for bloggers tend to be free. The sites Wordpress.com and Blogger.com are two of the most popular, but there are many others.

2. You may be tempted at first to play with colors and pictures and fonts and the other fancy enhancements the blogging software allows you to customize. Have fun with it but set yourself a limit on playing with those aspects that don't really matter. Good writing is what matters.

3. Some of the first bloggers had the goofy idea that a blog was a place where the writer just went online and talked about himself or herself all the time, like

a diary, or a therapist's couch. That's not interesting to anyone but the writer, in almost all cases, so it is by definition *not* good writing. A good blog should provide some focused information on the world (see #5 below), not just self-indulgent consideration of someone's daily minutiae.

4. Blogging is about sharing. Share the URL address of your blog at the bottom of every e-mail you send. Put it on your business card. If you write for a magazine or newsletter, put it in your author's bio. (My blog can be found at http://brevity.wordpress.com/.) Share space on your blog with other writers—institute a guest blogger of the week feature—and see if your guests will return the favor. Soon both of you will have an expanded readership. Share the names of blogs similar to your blog, and ask other's to share your information too. What we now call "the Internet" used to be called the World Wide Web, because it is a web of connections. Use it that way.

5. Want a successful blog, with many readers? The best advice is to choose a narrow subject area, something you know well or are eager to explore. "Thoughts from My Head," is too vague and unlikely to find an audience of any sort, while "Vegan Cooking for Picky Children" might be just what a number of people are looking for. (I discuss this a bit more in the section below.)

On Blogging, Platforms, and Book Deals

There is plenty of talk these days of people who landed book deals "based on their blog." The story goes like this: An agent or editor was just surfing the net one day, ran across a blog full of good writing, and said, "Wow! That'd make a great book." Then she picked up the phone. A new career was launched.

Does it happen?

Yes, it does, and has, and it will again. But consider it the longest of long shots. Like finding oil in your backyard.

Blogging can help your career in other ways, however.

The term "platform" is commonly used these days when discussing how one attracts the interest of a publisher. Honestly, the first time I heard this, I thought platform meant a large flat length of cardboard.

No, platform means soapbox. To put it simply, if you are going to write a book about a subject, a publisher is reassured if there are folks out there who already consider you an expert or authentic voice on the topic. A publisher wants books that sell, not books that sit in boxes in a warehouse.

At the extreme end, the importance of platform explains why folks who have their own cooking shows seem to have no trouble landing cookbook deals, why folks who offer therapeutic or diet advice on TV talk shows often produce multiple successful how-to books, and why late-night comics can publish a memoir about anything, anytime, with a big advance.

I'm guessing you are not a TV star, however, or a nationally acknowledged expert who gives forty-eight speeches a year to large groups.

In that case, a platform is something smaller, built slowly.

A blog as a platform works like this: You define a niche: Something everyday people need more information about. I can't tell you what that niche might be, because I don't know you or what makes you most curious and excited. And I can't tell you what might be most successful, because I don't know that either. (If I had a surefire million-dollar idea, I'd likely start that blog myself, wouldn't I?)

But I do know this: People flock to knitting blogs, to pet blogs focused on particular breeds (or particular health-related problems of specific breeds), to cooking blogs focused on local foods or special diets, to blogs that directly address

a) something people want to learn more about, or

b) something people are struggling over and need help with.

So let's say, for illustration, that your blog is entitled "Taming the Rambunctious Teenager." Maybe you have a background in counseling, or maybe you are just a tough-love mom with a great sense of humor and a clear-eyed way of describing your trials and tribulations with teenage drama. After you mention your blog on a few Internet discussion sites and share it with friends near and far by e-mail, a small group of people start to check in regularly, because some adolescent in their lives is driving them nuts, because your advice sounds helpful, and because the way you write about the problem brings people back for more.

Word of mouth kicks in. A few of your readers tell their friends, "You should read this." Some other parenting blogs mention your blog—"We just saw a great blog post on teenage tantrums over on 'Taming the Rambunctious Teenager'"—and they provide a link. People follow that link and like what they read.

Pretty soon, lots of folks are visiting, and lots of other sites link to your site.

That's suddenly a platform. While it remains highly un-likely that your Fairy Godmother will pop up at this point and make the rest of the process easy, you do now have something important with which to approach a publisher.

"Who would buy this book?" the publisher might ask.

"Well, I have three hundred readers who visit my blog regularly, just in the past year, and they will buy the book," you might answer. "And the fact that I found that many readers in just one year shows that this is a topic people care about, so I know there are thousands more readers for just this subject. And the fact that my blog is successful shows that I write about this topic in a way that people find helpful and appealing."

"Hmmm?" says the publisher, "let's talk."

RED LIGHT, GREEN LIGHT: TIPS FOR CONQUERING WRITER'S BLOCK

"What I try to do is write. I may write for two weeks 'the cat sat on the mat, that is that, not a rat.' And it might be just the most boring and awful stuff. But I try. When I'm writing, I write. And then it's as if the muse is convinced that I'm serious and says, 'Okay. Okay. I'll come.'"

—Maya Angelou

And now on to that pesky problem often called writer's block.

I'm not even sure, to be honest, that the thing exists. Sure, writers have bad days, and yes, they can occasionally have an entire series of bad days, but perhaps it comes down to definition. As I've said before, the bad days come with the good, and the moments where you are staring at your keyboard like a blockhead come right alongside the moments where your inner muse is throwing sentences at you faster than you can process them.

If you accept what I've said above (and in chapter nineteen), then the true definition of writer's block is when the writer gives up. If you walk away from the keyboard, the notepad, the desk, then yes, you are blocked, but it is of your own making. If you stay at the task, you aren't blocked, just idling for a while. Imagine yourself at a stoplight, waiting for the red circle to turn green.

But It Feels Like I'm Blocked

I don't mean to belittle how painfully difficult it is to sit at your writing desk through the unproductive moments or how long it might take for that wonderful green light to reappear. And yes, it does feel like a block some days. An insurmountable wall of cement blocks, actually.

So let's look at the source of the discomfort.

Writers block most often comes when the voices in our heads drown out our confidence. Maybe the voices insist:

- "My first sentence is so stupid I can't even imagine writing a second sentence," or

- "My ideas are dull, dull, dull, just like me," or

- "I don't have the vocabulary to make sentences that are fresh and writing that sounds intelligent, so why am I even bothering to try?" or,

- "My writing stinks to high heaven, in just about every way possible."

Believe me, if you've been at this writing vocation long enough, you've heard all of that from your internal voices and more. Even writers who have managed successful careers, published best-selling books, and have won acclaim and glowing reviews report those voices. They simply don't go away, in most cases.

So what's to be done?

Two things:

1. Expect the negative voices, and
2. Expect a lousy first draft.

Let me expand on these.

Expect the Negative Voices

The first step is to expect the voices and not be surprised, but also to not take them too seriously. Just because your internal writer's insecurity is telling you that "this work is not good enough, and there is no point in continuing such a fruitless enterprise," doesn't mean those voices must be heeded. You don't *have* to obey. Stopping the critical voices may be out of your control, but how you respond in the face of them *is* in your control.

My advice: Just say to yourself, "Oh, yeah, I've heard that before," and keep writing.

That makes it sound wonderfully easy, perhaps, and I'm not so "Susie Sunshine" as to suggest that this stubbornness in the face of discouragement isn't painfully difficult at times. But like so much else in life, ignoring these negative voices is a habit, and the more you deliberately practice a habit, the more routine it becomes. If you can work yourself into the habit of saying to yourself, "I'm feeling discouraged and uninspired today, but I'm just going to write some sentences anyway, and it doesn't even matter if they are bad sentences," you may find that writer's block becomes less and less of a factor in your writing life.

That last phrase, by the way—"... and it doesn't even matter if they are bad sentences ..."—is crucially important.

Bad sentences are not a problem, unless they remain on the page when the work is finished. Bad sentences that are later revised, however, are merely grist for the mill.

Or in other words: See the heading below.

Expect a Lousy First Draft

To my mind, the best way to avoid disappointment over what seems like a lousy attempt at an essay (or story or poem) is to fully expect a lousy first draft.

Personally, I never show anyone my first drafts, ever, under any circumstances. I can barely stand to look at them myself. My first (and sometimes second and third) drafts are filled with half-finished thoughts, summarized but unrealized ideas, halting steps, and glaring mistakes. Still, these drafts make me happy, because just filling the page with words is an accomplishment to be celebrated. I know that I can go back later and revise and improve those words, hone my thinking, compress my thoughts, until they seem wise and well structured.

It is a bit of a mind game, this business of expecting lousy early drafts so that you aren't disappointed when they inevitably come, but ask yourself:

Isn't this mental trick on yourself better than just sitting at your keyboard and staring at a blank page?

Isn't it better than giving up on your writing because you are worried that what comes out won't seem worthy enough to your internal critic?

Red Light, Green Light

Let me summarize my tips for waiting out the dry spells and getting that lingering red light to switch to a welcome green:

1. Know that it is normal. Everyone has bad days. So don't beat yourself up about it. There is nothing productive about beating up yourself up, and it doesn't feel good either.

2. The voices will come—"I'm a lousy writer, with dull ideas"—and though you can't make the voices go away in most cases, it is *entirely up to you what you do with them.* Obey them? Or just listen, shrug, and move forward?

3. If you stop writing for the day, the week, the month, your entire life, then the bad voices have won. Don't let that happen.

4. The key to handling the bad days and bad sentences is to love revision. How do you do that? Read the next chapter.

ON BECOMING AN EXCELLENT REWRITER

"I'm not a very good writer, but I'm an excellent rewriter."
—James Michener

Here's another bit of advice, simple but true: If you want to succeed as a writer, you must learn not only to revise, but to revise with vigor.

Just as successful painters work tirelessly on individual brushstrokes and the many other subtle techniques of oil painting or watercolor, and tennis stars work on backhand, forehand, ground stroke, volley, and lob, writers must work constantly to refine their word choice, sentence variety, paragraph structure, voice, persona—well, all of it.

Consider this advice from Mary Karr, author of the best-selling memoirs *The Liar's Club* and *Lit*:

> The truth is when I went to graduate school I would've said I was among the least talented of the students, I was certainly the least smart, or less educated. But I worked very hard. I worked very hard on these books, and one of the things I do is I rewrite, and rethink and reconsider. One reason I think people don't change things a lot is, I say to myself, is that true? Can I say that? Is

that right? And if I don't feel 100 percent certain
that I can I really try not to put it in.

So, if Mary Karr and James Michener only succeed by tireless rewriting, then who are we to try to do otherwise?

About Vigorous Revision

Most important is to first be sure that you understand the difference between copyediting and revision.

Imagine that your essay—maybe the third draft—is a living room in your suburban home, and you have decided to remodel that living room to make it into the best possible space it can be for relaxing and entertaining. Would you merely dust the end tables, adjust the angle of the lamp shades, and fluff up the sofa pillows? Well you might, but you wouldn't properly call that remodeling.

Likewise, trying to "revise" your essay by doing little more than correcting a few misplaced modifiers and sharpening up your sentence structure—while not wasted effort—is not revision, it is copyediting. And it is not enough.

What is required, if your essay and your writing skills are going to improve by leaps and bounds, is a total reconsideration of each and every element of your essay.

Let us return to that living room metaphor. If you are serious about remodeling, what you really need to do is to move each and every piece of furniture out onto the front lawn, roll up the area rugs, take the pictures down from the wall, perhaps even dismantle the outdated lighting fixtures, and then, on a case by case basis, decide what returns to the room and where it will be situated.

Sometimes a favorite table has to be left out on the curb for recycling, because it just doesn't fit anymore; maybe some new furniture is purchased (a new scene is written); perhaps the walls are painted a new color (voice or point-of-view shifts); or maybe all of the furniture is returned to the room but in a radically different configuration. What's important is that nothing goes back inside the metaphorical living room until and unless the remodeling homeowner makes the conscious choice that it belongs.

So, in a true revision of an essay, the same principle holds: Nothing remains in your essay—not the opening scene, not the funny anecdote in the middle, not your elegant closing paragraph—unless it serves the purpose of the essay that is taking shape on the page.

When to Revise

The truth is that most of us are constantly revising. We sound out the sentences in our head before we type them out onto the keyboard, and often we rearrange those very words a little as we stop to think what comes next. I've been known to revise sentences as I'm walking out to the garden to get lettuce and tomato for my lunch salad. A surprising number of writers report that they rewrite sentences and passages while in the shower. Maybe it's something about the water.

But vigorous revision—the stopping to move each piece of furniture out onto the lawn and deciding whether it really belongs—should come when your essay is beginning to reach some sense of cohesion. By that I mean that your essay, around the third or fourth draft, may be turning itself into something very different than the essay which you started. (Remember the idea that we don't really know our thoughts or feelings until we discover them in the act of writing?) It is not uncommon for me to be six or seven full drafts into an essay before I realize, "Aha, that's what this essay is going to be about."

After you start to see this central theme of your essay arise, what I like to call the magnetic core toward which each and every element of the essay is invisibly attracted, you should have that serious remodeling session.

Yes, the essay can meander, and yes, sometimes the wandering tangent is one of the most pleasurable parts of the essay for the reader, but each and every moment of the essay must still connect, even the digressions. When you think you see the core—for instance, this essay is about the loneliness I felt for years after the death of my brother, or this essay is looking at how country people relate differently to their neighbors than do city folk—then you can look at each and every sentence, paragraph, scene, and moment of reflection to see if it somehow reflects back to this magnetic center.

Have you ever read a work where everything seemed to fall magically into place, as if the thoughts that followed one upon another were inevitable, almost perfect in their sequence? Well trust me, the author's first draft was probably a jumbled mess of false starts and half-finished thoughts. That sense of inevitability and graceful perfection in the work came about because the writer you were reading struggled and struggled to find the perfect balance, never settling for less than the perfect note.

Listen to what essayist and short story writer Heather Sellers has said about revision:

> With each new version, I learn more about the truth of the piece, so I know which one to pick, which one is right, even if it's an early draft. Learning is a series of little improvements punctuated by many, many, many terrible disasters.

Or if that isn't strong enough for you, listen here to one of America's greatest writers, the immortal Mark Twain:

> The time to begin writing an article is when you have finished it to your satisfaction. By that time you begin to clearly and logically perceive what it is you really want to say.

Revising in Stages: The T.A. Approach

Another way of looking at revision, suggested to me years ago by the novelist and essayist David Bradley, has its roots in psychologist Eric Berne's ideas on Transactional Analysis, and his famous "parent adult child" theory.

Essentially, we all have three modes of thinking, described below, at our disposal.

The Child

The child is in the moment. He is fully engaged in seeing, hearing, feeling. Give a child a hunk of clay, and he will begin pushing on it, squeezing it, forming a ball, and then a snake, and then an elephant with a long, curly trunk, and he won't ask why. He is just absorbed in the doing.

The Adult

The adult *does* ask why, and makes logical choices. That hunk of clay needs to have a purpose, or why continue pushing at it?

The Parent

This is our ingrained voice of authority, absorbed from what was said to us repeatedly by parents and teachers when we were young. This is the (often shaming or critical) voice that suggests, "That looks more like a potato with a tail than it does an elephant," or "You just aren't good enough on the pottery wheel, and these vases will probably never earn you a dime."

If any psychologists are reading here, I admit to a loose, inelegant paraphrase of the more complex theory, but what I've said above is all you need to know in order to understand how this relates to writing.

When you begin a project, begin it with the Child attitude, pushing words around on the page, trying out ideas, doing those things that your fifth-grade writing teacher told you never to do, just to see what develops. Sentence fragment? Hey, it doesn't matter, as long as you are having fun. Allowing the Parent voice to enter into the process too soon is a form of writer's block and can shut down the enterprise entirely. You need to be open to any option, with almost no goal in mind.

At some point however, the writer *does* need to allow the Adult to enter the discussion. "Okay," that Adult internal voice may suggest, "what exactly are you up to here? Is this an essay, a piece of memoir, a spiritual travelogue? Who do I think will read this? What do they need to know about me and my experience to even follow my thoughts?" This more directive mode of thinking about the writing at hand may occur maybe three or five drafts into a project and continue through multiple additional drafts. It is highly useful to ask these sorts of questions at the appropriate time.

The Parent voice, however, should be held at bay until the very end of the process of writing and revision. The Parent voice is the one most likely to criticize, make you feel inadequate, or point out what's expected of you in society. This voice might ask, "Are you going to let everyone at church see you in that faded blouse?" or "Why can't you be like your sister Louise? She always writes tantalizing metaphors."

Comments like these—I'll call them confidence destroyers—aren't useful, of course, at least not when expressed so negatively. But if you turn those questions around, they *do* become helpful. At the very end of writing and revising, just at the moment when you are about to print your essay and put it in an envelope for the magazine you have chosen as the best possible market, or just before you submit it to your writing group, or post it on your blog, ask yourself, "Is every sentence polished, crisp, and exactly what I want to say?" and "Are my metaphors fresh, clear, and accurate? Each and every one?"

Each of these three aspects of yourself—childish wonder, adult logic, and parental concern—are gifts you can use to make your writing stronger. The trick, you see, is all in the timing.

ON PUBLICATION, REJECTION, AND BEING STUBBORN

"I've been rejected thousands of times. You have to accept that as part of the arrangement, and allow it to make you more humble—and stubborn to succeed."
—Steve Almond

My first book had only been available for about a week when I drove into Philadelphia for my initial bookstore reading, the preliminary leg of a very modest—meaning no limo driver and no expense account—book tour. Still, despite the lack of airplane rides or five-star hotels, I was excited. Years of dreaming and hard work had led to this moment.

My publisher had hooked me up with a long-standing, well-respected independent bookstore in center city, though in retrospect someone should have checked to see how the shop had been doing "lately."

I admit to a measure of dismay when the manager met me in an ill-fitting, pilled sweater at the front of an empty store and then walked me up a flight of steps to a narrow, dingy second floor. It wasn't the small number of cheap folding chairs that caught me up short, or the rickety podium. It was the vast array of "gently used" pornographic books and magazines that lined the walls. Though the main floor of this once-thriving bookshop contained the finest contemporary and classic literature, it seems the second-story skin books were paying the electric bills.

I won't dwell on the disappointing details of what followed. It was simple: No one came. Okay, one personal friend and his wife showed up a bit late, but they were also friends of the bookstore owner, so it is hard to say if they were there to see me, to see him, or to have a glass of wine, which is what we did when it became apparent that my reading was a total bust.

Live and learn, I thought. Maybe Sunday is a bad day for a bookstore reading. Maybe bookstore readings don't sell books. Maybe every author faces an empty room when trying to do a bookstore appearance.

I tried every justification to bolster my flagging spirits as I walked back to my sister-in-law's apartment that Sunday afternoon, down Walnut Street, toward Rittenhouse Square, where I hoped to grab a cup of coffee and just forget it all

But I saw the dang-blasted line a half block away. Hundreds of young couples, many, but not all, with strollers or toddlers, snaking along the sidewalk, into the sparkling new Borders bookstore, the one with the comfy chairs and coffee shop. I had to walk right by the line, and then, as if there was a lesson to be learned, I had to walk in, to see the line snake all around the first floor of the chain bookstore, up the steps, and once more around the second floor, until it ended at a wide table, where children's author Chris Van Allsburg, flanked by four store employees, was signing copies of *The Polar Express*.

Thousands of copies.

He seemed very nice.

Perseverance Furthers

Aside from being a funny story to tell my friends—especially those friends who are discouraged when their first poem, essay, story, or book doesn't seem to get as much notice as they had fantasized—the story is also useful to illustrate the importance of obstinacy and perseverance.

Though for a day or two I was tempted to write about nothing but polar bears and arctic trains for the rest of my career, what I eventually did with this experience was return to my desk and write five more books. None of them has been as wildly successful as Allsburg's picture books (and, by the way, he deserves the success), but I'm still here, still plugging.

Now some of you are probably thinking, "That's easy for Dinty to say. He's publishing his books. I'm still waiting to publish my first essay, and those two rejection letters last month really hurt."

Trust me, I've received over five hundred rejection letters in my writing life—and I still receive them, of course. And yes, my gut sinks every time I open one. But had I stopped writing stories and essays after the first fifteen rejections or so, where would I be now? Still nursing my wounds, unpublished, and wondering what might have been.

As author Steve Almond says in the quotation that begins this chapter, you must allow these rejection moments "to make you more humble—and stubborn to succeed."

On Loving What You Do

So, if you do get stubborn, what do you need to know about the ways and means and inner workings of publishing your own writing?

Crafting the Personal Essay

Well first, you have to love the work itself. If you don't truly enjoy moving words and sentences around on the page—similar to the way you delighted in moving wooden blocks and plastic trucks around on the living room carpet when you were five—then you are going to have a hard time persevering through the ups and downs and inevitable setbacks.

I have had students in my classes over the years who didn't take pleasure in the act of writing but somehow got it into their heads that it would be fulfilling and wonderful to *have written*, to be a published writer. Well, it does feel good, but I'm not a big fan of putting the cart before the horse.

Yes, every writer has bad days, slow stretches, but if you don't have days when the writing itself is its own reward, when you would do it even if there was no such thing as a magazine, book publisher, or reader, then you may want to reexamine why you are trying at all.

Assuming that you are a writer who likes to write, one who feels the thrill and energy of finally getting an idea clear on the page or carefully crafting the perfect scene, then the next thing you need to do is stop thinking about rejection *or* acceptance.

Novelist Barbara Kingsolver says it very well:

> Close the door. Write with no one looking over your shoulder. Don't try to figure out what other people want to hear from you; figure out what you have to say. It's the one and only thing you have to offer.

What to Know About Submitting Your Work

The first and best advice on the process of submitting and finding your work published is found in the two chapters before the one you are reading now. You must cultivate a practice of careful writing and vigorous, painstaking revision to make sure the piece you submit is as absolutely crisp, fresh, and flawless as can be. The competition is doing this, so you need to do so as well.

Here are some additional guidelines to save effort and increase your chances at success:

- **Know your magazine:** Editors have often expressed grief over the wasted paper and postage (and time) when work is submitted that simply does not fit the guidelines. Even if your essay was the finest ever written in the history of letters, there is no chance of seeing it published in a literary magazine that publishes only poems. That one is pretty obvious, though you might be surprised how many folks still get it wrong. More subtle is whether the magazine in question only publishes prose of a certain length, or whether it focuses on work that promotes Christian values, or whether the periodical is or is not willing to consider work with a particular political slant. Some magazines want only stories about rural life, while others insist on a hip, urban voice. You can learn about magazines—what they desire in terms of genre, in terms of length, in terms of subject matter, and how they want submissions to arrive—by reading books such as *Writer's Market*, by studying the magazines themselves in the library and bookstores, or by requesting sample issues. The time this takes will be well worth it in the long run.

- **Keep your cover letter simple:** It is customary to attach a short cover letter to the front of your manuscript (though even this is changing some with electronic submission systems). The cover letter should be brief and to the point. "Dear Editor (or Editor's Name), Enclosed is my essay entitled "The Essay," which I hope you will find suitable for publication in your magazine. I have been reading *Well-Respected Magazine* for many years now and am always delighted by the range of intelligent nonfiction I find within the pages. My work has been previously published in *Small Magazine* and *Very Small Literary Journal.* If you decide not to publish my work, please recycle the manuscript and use the enclosed SASE (self-addressed stamped envelope) to let me know your decision. Sincerely, I.M.A. Writer."

- **Let the Work Do the Talking:** You may note that the sample cover letter above doesn't describe the content of the submission or try to convince the editor of the essay's merit. That's because the work itself has to convince the editor, and if the work needs to be described and explained in the cover letter, it is likely not clearly enough written. One exception might be if you are writing an essay about the birth of a lamb and want to point out that you were a sheep farmer for twenty years. Or if you are writing about issues related to children with autism and felt it helpful to mention your own experience as the mother of a child with autistic disorder. Background information on the author is sometimes useful, but don't try to sell your work the way someone might pitch a movie or sell a car. And whatever you do, don't include confetti stars, glitter hearts, or pictures of your two cats in your submission envelope. That marks you as an amateur, and editors are looking for serious, seasoned writers, not gimmickry.

- **Use Plain Jane formatting:** Use black ink, a clear and common font (12 point Times New Roman is the most often used), and margins of about 1 inch on all sides. Double-space your manuscript and print on only one side of the paper. At the top of the first page of your manuscript show your name, your e-mail address, your mailing address, your phone number, and a word count. Page numbers are usually appreciated.

- **Eliminate all grammatical and spelling errors:** Even if you aren't gifted in this area, you can buy lunch for a friend who has an eagle eye and good spelling skills in return for a thorough copyedit. Editors often review hundreds of manuscripts a week, and you don't want to annoy them or make them impatient. Would you show up at a job interview with your shirt buttons undone and your belt unclasped?

- **Avoid carpet bombing:** The successful authors I know send work to selected magazines and journals, based on their understanding of the submission guidelines and editorial needs. They don't mail off forty copies of an essay to every magazine imaginable. Choose your targets wisely. And if an editor sends you a polite note asking "to see more work," don't send everything you've ever written back in a cardboard box. Choose wisely and judiciously here

Crafting the Personal Essay

as well. When you send only your *best* work, the odds of acceptance go up considerably.

- **Put Rejections in Perspective:** When you do—and inevitably you will—receive that cold, discouraging rejection slip, feel free to have the inevitable emotional reaction, but then let the more rational part of your brain process what has occurred. There are really two choices here, and either one is as possible as the other. Work gets rejected because it is not good enough (yet), because the author sees clearly what she is up to and what she is trying to convey but has not found a way to include the reader in on these moments (and editors are the stingiest, pickiest of readers). If that is the case, then put the writing aside for a week or so before attacking it with fresh eyes. You *can* make it better. But work is sometimes rejected because a particular editor just wasn't the right set of eyes for your writing, or the magazine has been inundated lately with more good work than it can handle. Don't assume the editor is always right, and don't let a rejection slow you down. Learn to view your own work honestly and clearly, and you'll know which choice to make.

APPENDIX A:
"OF IDLE PEOPLE WHO ROVE ABOUT"

BY DINTY W. MOORE

I arrived in Boca Raton as naïve as Christopher Columbus when he first stumbled off the Santa Maria thinking he had landed on East Indian shores. I had visions of walking along serene Boca beaches, of pearly shells crunching under foot, of dolphins leaping in a golden sunset, and of encountering the occasional native Floridian under a palm tree to exchange pleasantries about idyllic life in a slow-paced beachfront paradise.

Of course, I knew nothing.

And as for paradise, I hope never to return.

> *Two or three hours' walking will carry me to as strange*
> *a country as I expect ever to see.*

My first full day in Boca, a Monday, I set out early to meet my afternoon class at Florida Atlantic University. I was the guest writer for the week, and eager to make the acquaintance of my new charges.

The evening before, I dismissed a possible warning from Nicole, the graduate student who kindly rescued me at the Ft. Lauderdale airport.

"I enjoy a good walk," I insisted when she offered to re-trieve me from my hotel lobby each day and deliver me di-rectly to campus. "It's only about a mile, right?"

"But I'm *happy* to pick you up," Nicole repeated, an odd, almost sad, tone in her voice.

"I'll be fine," I offered breezily. "Just fine."

The simple mile, a mere stroll for someone who enjoys walking as much as I enjoy walking, ran almost entirely along Glades Road, a six-lane highway whose main purpose, it turns out, is to funnel thousands of automobiles every fifteen minutes or so onto, off of, and over I-95.

The storied interstate runs from the northern tip of Maine to just south of Miami, passing through fifteen sepa-rate states along the way, skirting major metropolitan cen-ters such as Boston, New York, Philadelphia, and Baltimore, finally bisecting Florida like a rigid spine of concrete and carbon monoxide.

At the point that I-95 runs under Glades Road, passing through the heart of Boca, the interstate has ten lanes, and for most of my walk that Monday morning I was dodging entrance ramps, exit ramps, and scores of impatient driv-ers scowling behind tinted windows. They were clearly an-noyed that this man, this pedestrian, this fellow without enough sense to find a proper wheeled-vehicle, was just slowing everything down. Some drivers gave me the right-of-way, most did not, but it seemed as if none of them were pleased, or for that matter, accustomed to someone crossing the off-ramps on foot. I was a pesky distraction to the usual morning routine.

But being made of stronger stock than most, instead of curling into a fetal ball alongside the fourth on-ramp, disap-pearing myself into the bushes together with the discarded fast-food wrappers, beer cans, and condoms, I plunged forward, across the concrete circles-of-hell, toward what my map told me would be the entrance to the FAU campus.

I had pictured—being the sort of fellow who visits college campuses with some regularity—that I would hit upon a more foot-friendly territory near the campus, a lively area, perhaps, peppered with carefree undergraduates, a few hackie-sacking slackers, some engineering majors staring into laptops outside a coffee shop, and a bar, certainly, or six of them, since students tend toward Herculean thirst. Along with this, I imagined a campus gate, a red-brick sidewalk, some sort of feline mascot in stone, and some easy, inviting way for those of us inclined to perambulation to find our way onto the campus grounds.

Poor naïve me.

Instead, what I found, in the bright white heat of Florida in April, was perhaps the most difficult intersection of all. I literally had to sprint across ten lanes of Glades Road (expanded at this point to allow for multiple turning lanes) in the small amount of time allotted in the red-yellow-green light system, and still, I was the only poor soul on foot.

I survived, to find a campus—not surprisingly, in retrospect—ringed by parking, and a friendly enough student union, where I secured a cold sports drink and calmed my nerves.

> We should go forth on the shortest walk, perchance, in
> the spirit of undying adventure, never to return, pre-
> pared to send back our embalmed hearts only as relics
> to our desolate kingdoms.

Having grasped that the I-95 overpass was not pedestrian friendly, despite the misleading sidewalks, I secured a bus schedule and a better map on Tuesday, and planned an outing to the Atlantic Ocean, about four miles down the road.

Did the bus run to the ocean?

Of course not.

Boca's bus system connects shopping mall to medical complex to shopping mall, and not for the patrons mind you, because anyone who can afford to shop at the high-end stores of the Boca Raton Town Center Mall obviously owns more than one car.

Judging from the weary looks of my fellow bus patrons, the bus system exists primarily to ferry those hardworking folks who wash the floors, empty the trash, and watch the night for the various commercial establishments along the way.

The closest the bus would take me to water was a stop at the Publix Super Market, about 1.2 miles away. Late that afternoon, I cheerfully stepped off the bus and headed east, toward the smell of water and the shriek of gulls.

And what I saw were homes, beautiful homes, walled homes, windows closed, shutters drawn, the occasional Cadillac Escalante parked in an immaculate driveway, manicured shrubs, ornamental bushes, warning signs on every lawn—"Alarm System installed"—and cars, whizzing past in every direction.

What I didn't see: birds, squirrels, children, elderly folks out for a stroll, people in their driveways, people on porches enjoying the day, folks walking to the corner market for a quart of milk, or anyone on foot.

Except when I reached the causeway, a drawbridge set in place to let the massive yachts and sailboats into Lake Boca Raton, where I saw a young man of twenty or so, likely of Mexican or Central American descent, down by the water with a four-foot iguana on a leash. The iguana was swimming, and the young man was holding the lizard's tether along the bank of the inlet.

I couldn't get close enough to the young man to speak with him, so I waved.

He waved back with his free hand.

> *I have met with but one or two persons in the course of my life who understood the art of Walking, that is, of taking walks—who had a genius, so to speak, for sauntering, which word is beautifully derived "from idle people who roved about the country, in the Middle Ages, and asked charity, under pretense of going a la Sainte Terre," to the Holy Land, till the children exclaimed, "There goes a Sainte-Terrer," a Saunterer, a Holy-Lander.*

"You walked? You actually walked?"

My students were incredulous. One or two gave me a look suggesting that I perhaps had a screw or three loose in my head. I had not only on the previous day walked from the Publix to the beach, maybe twenty minutes past those rows of desolate mansions, but then I walked from the ocean back to my hotel, another ninety minutes or so.

This was after some difficulty actually finding the ocean, because it was entirely hidden behind high-rise apartment building and condos, all of which announced: "Beach Access for Residents Only." The beach, by law, is free for everyone. You just aren't allowed to cross anyone's property to get there.

"No one walks in Boca Raton," my students laughed, when I told my story.

"You could have been killed."

Crafting the Personal Essay

"I sure wouldn't walk here."

"Damn. I *wouldn't* live here."

And it hit me then, in the wonderful way that hindsight suddenly makes sense of disparate confusions: None of these students lived in Boca. FAU exists only because I-95 provides such easy vehicular access to a student body spread up and down the Miami–Port St. Lucie corridor. Boca is just a resort town for the wealthy and the retired.

(Supposedly for drug money as well, though that oft-repeated claim may be apocryphal. If I wanted to hide a drug operation, however, and could afford it, Boca would be the perfect solution: No one snoops around on the sidewalks, neighbors never come to the fence, everyone's home is walled, and driving an SUV the size of a dump truck attracts absolutely no attention.)

But back to my main point.

My FAU student friends live wherever they can afford to live, and that's certainly not Boca. They drive in to campus every day, take a class or two, and then rush off to (often full-time) jobs, twelve or twenty exits up or down the interstate. No one but the fool that is me would actually imagine walking to this campus.

> My vicinity affords many good walks; and though for
> so many years I have walked almost every day, and
> sometimes for several days together, I have not yet ex-
> hausted them. An absolutely new prospect is a great
> happiness, and I can still get this any afternoon.

Like all deeply ingrained habits, my sauntering began early, in grade school. I didn't walk twenty miles through chest-deep snow in bare feet, but I did walk a half-a-mile each day, rain or shine, and we lived along the Lake Erie snow belt. This remains one of my fondest memories of childhood.

There was, indeed, a candy store along the way, and though the Sisters of St. Joseph would certainly not allow us to eat penny candy during class, you could circumvent the prohibition with a five-cent box of Smith Brothers cherry cough drops, which were nothing more than cherry candy in disguise, and a fake cough. My classmates also lived along the route, and sometimes we would randomly meet up at the corner of Eighth and Cranberry, other times we would knock on one another's doors and join up on purpose, and occasionally we would take a wide detour to avoid one another.

Walking home was even better, because there was no time limit, no opening bell. So I could wander, often alone, sometimes with a buddy, up and down the odd avenues, past the excitable dog behind the rusted fence, into the woods that bordered Sixth Street, down to Frontier Creek to float leaf boats, or past the house that contained a feral, hair-covered, criminally insane thirty-year-old "wolf man" chained to a wall. We spent a fair amount of time trying to catch a glimpse of this poor fellow in the tiny attic window of the decrepit house, but oddly, no one ever reported a credible sighting.

These walks, to and from school, are how I learned the patterns of my neighborhood, the habits of the people, the comings and goings of the man who actually wore a suit to work every day, the family that gathered around the piano to sing songs before dinner, the foreign woman whose front porch smelled liked cooked cabbage, the housewife who was always rushing off in her car with an angry look in her eyes, the young couple with what we then called a "retarded

Crafting the Personal Essay

child," the elderly man who took ten minutes just to walk around his own house.

You come to care about a place when you know it this intimately, when you see the patterns, and discern the subtle changes. One day the elderly man was no longer taking his morning walk. The poor family in the ratty duplex disappeared overnight, the front porch littered with whatever didn't fit into the back of the truck. There was a window broken on the angry woman's car, and two weeks later she was gone as well.

Me thinks that the moment my legs begin to move, my thoughts begin to flow.

I live in a small college town in Appalachian Ohio, and I often walk to work.

It takes me forty-five minutes, which can be tiring at times, but the more I do it the quicker the time goes by. For a while, I had an argument running in my head: You could get more work done, write more essays, clear more e-mails from your inbox, if you didn't spend ninety minutes walking to and from campus. But then I realized I did get more work done on the days that I walked, because I was sharper, clearer, had used some of the foot-time to sort the detritus from my brain and identify the daily to-do list that actually mattered.

And what I really like about walking to work is that I see people.

There is a woman, a nurse who I imagine works the overnight shift, because I see her in her front garden often in the late morning, still wearing her medical smock. I complimented her on her roses one day, and she beamed. Now we wave and smile every once in a while.

Two weeks back, I spotted a bird, obviously young and just fallen from a tree, on the front lawn of a student apartment house. Two college kids—modern-day hippie types—were sitting on the porch, so I pointed out the bird to them. The young man, dreadlocked and tie-dyed, stopped everything, tied up his dog who was suddenly curious as well, and rescued the bird.

There is an overweight gentleman who spends every afternoon on a porch swing, and we nod and smile regularly. There are regular joggers who seem to really like that I step aside onto the grass when they come up to me, so they can stay on the sidewalk, where there is less chance they will turn an ankle. There are these guys who have been sandblasting all of the paint from a beautiful but down-and-out Victorian house for months, and every once in a while I mention that the project is coming along well. They seem to appreciate it.

The notion that our cities and towns are losing any sense of community, that neighborhoods are no longer places where one family looks out for another and everyone feels safe, that neighbors don't even know the names of the folks right next door, is widespread, oft-cited in newspaper editorials, listed as either symptom or cause of any number of social ills. We shake our heads and sadly wonder what has gone wrong.

Hey, we aren't helping each other here!

Get out of the damn car and walk around.

Get to know your street, the street behind you, and the people up and down your block.

When sometimes I am reminded that the mechanics and shopkeepers stay in their shops not only all the forenoon, but all the afternoon too, sitting with

crossed legs, so many of them—as if the legs were
made to sit upon, and not to stand or walk upon—I
think that they deserve some credit for not having all
committed suicide long ago.

Henry David Thoreau, author of the occasional quotes embedded in this essay, didn't live to see the automobile.

That's probably a good thing. He was cranky enough.

Suicide, he says? People forced to sit all day in offices, stores, and cubicles should be commended for not taking their own lives?

Perhaps he was just exaggerating for effect. Writers have been known to do that.

Or maybe he truly believed what he wrote. Perhaps he saw what I began to see as I persisted in my vain attempts to saunter through Boca Raton, to find some heart to that unapproachable community, to claim some small corner for the humble foot soldier against the unwelcoming intersections and ubiquitous automobile.

The fact that no one but me was out and about, that no one else was strolling along the sidewalks, working in their side yards, trimming the yellow roses, throwing Frisbees, or walking wiener dogs on their stubby little legs, combined with those grand, sprawling homes all shuttered, air-conditioned, set off by fences and inhospitable gates, put me to mind of mausoleums or Egyptian pyramids. These would be grand structures in which to be entombed, really, but there is time enough for that *after* death.

And now maybe I'm the one exaggerating for effect, but just as being shut away in one of these hermetically sealed homes, surrounded by nothing but television and burglar alarms, seems something like a premature burial, the prospect of living your days inside of an automobile is not much to be preferred.

In death, our souls are transported, though we do not know in precisely what fashion. In Boca, our souls are transported, by sports cars with spoked rims and tinted windows.

Either way, that's not quite living.

My apologies to Mr. Thoreau. Perhaps I'm the cranky one.

But here's the simple truth:

When I'm sauntering, wandering, strolling, ambling, rambling, bopping along on two sturdy feet, I'm much more optimistic. I feel entirely alive.

APPENDIX B:

RECOMMENDED READINGS FOR WRITERS

"Reading is to the mind what exercise is to the body."
—Joseph Addison

Writers never exist in a vacuum, and this is especially true in the nonfiction form. The successful essayist finds nourishment in the world around her, but also in a wide-ranging menu of satisfying reading. In order to grow as a writer, you need to explore the work of other essayists, study what they do best (or where they go astray), and learn from that work.

Writers, of course, find all sort of reading useful, including books on science, politics, art and architecture, and the ingredients of *Bún bò Huế*. The more you experience, and the more you understand about the world, the better you will be at finding and exploring connections.

In her book *The Creative Habit: Learn It and Use It for Life,* the dancer and choreographer Twyla Tharp puts the point this way:

> The great painters are incomparable draftsmen.
> They also know how to mix their own paint, grind
> it, put in the fixative; no task is too small to be

> worthy of their attention. The great composers
> are usually dazzling musicians. ... A great chef can
> chop and dice better than anyone in the kitchen.
> The best fashion designers are invariably virtuo-
> sos with a needle and thread ... The best writers
> are well-read people. They have the richest ap-
> preciation of words, the biggest vocabularies, the
> keenest ear for language.

So, like so many other writers have done before me, I enthusiastically recommend reading good books of all sorts,
as often as possible.

Here are a few of my overall favorites, in the nonfiction
essay form:

James Baldwin, *Notes of a Native Son*

Joan Didion, *The White Album*

Joan Didion, *Slouching Towards Bethlehem*

Ted Kooser, *Local Wonders: Seasons in the Bohe-
mian Alps*

George Orwell, *A Collection of Essays*

Richard Rodriguez, *Hunger of Memory: The Education of Richard Rodriguez*

Scott Russell Sanders, *A Private History of Awe*

Floyd Skloot, *In the Shadow of Memory*

Abigail Thomas, *Safekeeping: Some True Stories
from a Life*

Terry Tempest Williams, *Finding Beauty in a Broken World*

The Best American Essays (Annual Anthology), edited by Robert Atwan

The Best Creative Nonfiction (Annual Anthology), edited by Lee Gutkind

Here, too, are some recommended books focused on the various subgenres of the essay:

The Memoir Essay

Jo Ann Beard, *The Boys of My Youth*

Bob Cowser, Jr., *Scorekeeping: Essays From Home*

Sonja Livingston, *Ghostbread*

Ira Sukrungruang, *Talk Thai: The Adventures of Buddhist Boy*

The Contemplative Essay

William Hazlitt, *Selected Writings*

Phillip Lopate, *Against Joie de Vivre*

Patrick Madden, *Quotidiana*

Virginia Woolf, *Moments of Being*

The Lyric Essay

Lia Purpura, *On Looking*

Kim Dana Kupperman, *I Just Lately Started Buying Wings: Missives from the Other Side of Silence*

Brenda Miller, *Blessing of the Animals*

Naomi Shihab Nye, *Never in a Hurry: Essays on People and Places*

The Spiritual Essay

Brian Doyle, *Leaping: Revelations & Epiphanies*

Anne Lamott, *Traveling Mercies: Some Thoughts on Faith*

Clark Strand, *Meditation Without Gurus: A Guide to the Heart of Practice*

The Best American Spiritual Writing, (Annual Anthology), edited by Philip Zaleski

The Gastronomical Essay

M.F.K. Fisher, *The Art of Eating*

Eric LeMay, *Immortal Milk*

Calvin Trillin, *Feeding a Yen: Savoring Local Specialties, from Kansas City to Cuzco*

Best Food Writing, (Annual Anthology), edited by Holly Hughes

The Humorous Essay

Robert Benchley, *My Ten Years in a Quandary and How They Grew*

Robin Hemley, *Do-Over! In which a forty-eight-year-old father of three returns to kindergarten, summer camp, the prom, and other embarrassments*

Dorothy Parker, *The Portable Dorothy Parker*

David Sedaris, *Me Talk Pretty One Day*

The Nature Essay

Marcia Bonta, *Appalachian Spring, Appalachian Summer, Appalachian Autumn, Appalachian Winter*

Barbara Hurd, *Stirring the Mud: On Swamps, Bogs, and Human Imagination*

Barry Lopez, *About This Life: Journeys on the Threshold of Memory*

The Best American Science and Nature Writing (Annual Anthology), edited by Tim Folger

The Travel Essay

Bruce Chatwin, *In Patagonia*

Pico Iyer, *The Global Soul: Jet Lag, Shopping Malls, and the Search for Home*

Rolf Potts, *Marco Polo Didn't Go There: Stories and Revelations from One Decade as a Postmodern Travel Writer*

Kira Salak, *Four Corners: A Journey into the Heart of Papua New Guinea*

And finally, here are some excellent books on the craft of writing:

Judith Barrington, *Writing the Memoir: From Truth to Art*

Sherry Ellis (ed.), *Now Write! Nonfiction: Memoir, Journalism and Creative Nonfiction Exercises from Today's Best Writers*

Philip Gerard, Carolyn Forché (eds.), *Writing Creative Nonfiction*

Natalie Goldberg, *Writing Down the Bones*

Vivian Gornick, *The Situation and the Story*

Lee Gutkind, *Keep It Real: Everything You Need to Know About Researching and Writing Creative Nonfiction*

Anne Lamott, *Bird by Bird: Some Instructions on Writing and Life*

Rebecca McClanahan, *Write Your Heart Out*

Flannery O'Connor, *The Habit of Being*

Bill Roorbach, *Writing Life Stories: How To Make Memories Into Memoirs, Ideas Into Essays and Life Into Literature*

Heather Sellers, *Page After Page*

Sue William Silverman, *Fearless Confessions: A Writer's Guide to Memoir*

Feel free to pick and choose from my lists, but ultimately the goal is to create your own list and find nourishment from it each and every day.

APPENDIX C:

WEB SITES FOR ESSAY WRITERS

"Publishing online is often free, easy to access, and sometimes more popular than many print literary journals. But some literary critics continue to deride online publishing as not the 'real thing.'"
—Julie Dolan, *Utne.com*

While books—in whatever form they exist now or might exist in the future—will always remain important to writers and readers, there is no arguing that technology is opening up new venues for the written word. Initially, as reflected in the quote topping this chapter, online publishing was seen as a home for bad writing—the place for amateurs. But all of that has changed and continues to change, as more and more serious readers and talented writers discover the countless benefits of low-cost, instant-access global publishing platforms.

In addition to the growing array of Web sites where serious writers can publish their work, there are also countless Web sites that assist writers with learning about craft, finding prompts and inspiration, and doing research.

A brief roundup of such sites can be found below. But a quick note of warning: Don't let the endless resources distract you from writing. The Web is wonderful in that it is virtually endless, so it is up to us to switch off the browser when we find ourselves in "mindless surfing" mode, and get back to the business at hand: writing, and writing well.

Online Magazines That Publish Essays

The reason that online magazines were once seen as less serious than "ink and paper" magazines is tied to the ease of distribution and low cost. Early on in the growth of on-line publishing, many Web-based literary magazines found themselves publishing almost everything that was submitted. Once a Web site domain was purchased (and, actually, many companies gave them away for free), there were no paper costs, no printing costs, no mailing costs, so the size of the magazine wasn't a factor. The editors did not need to be picky. Thus, hundreds of magazines sprung up where the editors essentially just published five or twenty of their friends in each issue, and then folded after issue two.

The instinct was good—generosity and helping beginning writers are not bad things—but the strategy backfired. There were so many Internet magazines publishing so many unedited, careless works of poetry, fiction, and nonfiction that the audience was turned away.

Now, a decade into the twenty-first century, a cadre of professionally edited, discerning online magazines has been established to prove that Web-based literary outlets can be every bit as serious as their venerable paper counterparts.

Here are a few I consider especially worth reading (and when you think you work is ready, also submitting):

- *Blackbird*   www.blackbird.vcu.edu

- *Born Magazine*   www.bornmagazine.org

- *Brevity*   www.creativenonfiction.org/brevity

- *Connotation Press*   www.connotationpress.com

- *Diagram*   www.thediagram.com

- *Drunken Boat*   www.thedrunkenboat.com

- *Evergreen Review*   www.evergreenreview.com

- *Failbetter*   www.failbetter.com/index.php

- *Guernica*   www.guernicamag.com

- *McSweeney's*   www.mcsweeneys.net

- *Mississippi Review Online*   www.mississippireview.com

- *Narrative*   www.narrativemagazine.com

- *Nidus*   www.pitt.edu/~nidus

- *Pif Magazine*   www.pifmagazine.com

- *Qarrtsiluni*   www.qarrtsiluni.com

- *Quay*   www.quayjournal.org

- *Sweet*   www.sweetlit.com

- *Terrain.org*   www.terrain.org

Web Sites of Traditional Magazines That Publish Essays

Many traditional "ink and paper" magazines also publish essays. These range from well-known, high-paying (and hard-to-break-into) markets like Oprah's *O* magazine, *Harper's*, *The Atlantic*, and *The New York Times Sunday Magazine*, to more modest literary magazines. Many of the latter offer a significant Web presence to go along with their paper issues, and a few of the best known are listed here:

Nonfiction Only

- *Creative Nonfiction*   www.creativenonfiction.org
- *Fourth Genre*   www.msupress.msu.edu/journals/fg
- *River Teeth*   http://muse.jhu.edu/journals/river_teeth

Multigenre (Nonfiction, Fiction, and Poetry) Magazines

- *Arts & Letters*   http://al.gcsu.edu
- *Iowa Review*   www.uiowa.edu/~iareview
- *Missouri Review Online*   www.missourireview.org
- *New Ohio Review*   www.ohio.edu/nor
- *Ploughshares*   www.pshares.org
- *Prairie Schooner*   www.prairieschooner.unl.edu
- *The Normal School*   www.thenormalschool.com
- *Tin House*   www.tinhouse.com

Useful Web Sites for Writers

And of course, the Web offers myriad resources helpful for research, organization, encouragement, and community. A full listing would probably double the size of this book, but here are some good ones to at least get you started, including *The Writer's Digest* site and Web sites for Writers, both offering links to many, many more excellent resources:

- *Association of Writer's and Writing Programs*   www. awpwriter.org

- *Poynter Online*   www.poynter.org

- *Purdue Online Writing Lab*   http://owl.english.purdue.edu

- *Shaw Guides to Writers Conferences*   www.writing.shawguides.com

- *Websites for Writers*   www.websitesforwriters.net

- *Writer Beware*   www.accrispin.blogspot.com

- *Writer's Digest*   www.writersdigest.com

- *Writer's Market*   www.writersmarket.com

- *WritingFix*   www.writingfix.com

permissions

"Ah, Wilderness! Humans, Hawks, and Environmental Correctness on the Muddy Rio Grande," by Dinty W. Moore, first appeared in *Arts & Letters: Journal of Contemporary Culture*. Copyright © 1999 by Dinty W. Moore. Reprinted by permission of the author.

Excerpts from "Beauty," © 1998 by Scott Russell Sanders; first published in *Orion*; collected in the author's *Hunting for Hope* (Beacon Press, 1998): Reprinted by permission of the author.

Excerpts from "Glaciology," by Lia Purpura, from *On Looking: Essays*. Copyright © 2006 by Lia Purpura. Reprinted by permission of the author and Sarabande Books, www. sarabandebooks.org.

Excerpts from "Mr. Secrets," by Richard Rodriguez, from *Hunger of Memory: The Education of Richard Rodriguez*. Reprinted by permission of David R. Godine, Publisher, Inc. Copyright © 1982 by Richard Rodriguez.

"Of Idle People Who Rove About," By Dinty W. Moore. Copyright © 2010 by Dinty W. Moore. Reprinted by permission of the author.

"Pulling Teeth, or 20 Reasons Why My Daughter Turning 20 Can't Come Soon Enough," by Dinty W. Moore, first appeared in *Gulf Coast*. Copyright © 2008 by Dinty W. Moore. Reprinted by permission of the author.

index

acknowledgments

All that I know about writing, editing, and teaching is the result of the numerous writers, teachers, students, and editors who have patiently worked with me over the past twenty-five years. The simplest truth is that to be a writer means to grow stronger and clearer in the art and craft of writing each day, and that can only be done by sharing and discussing with other committed, intelligent people.

So I am thankful to countless folks, including Lee Gutkind, Hattie Fletcher, Richard Rubin, Rodger Kamenetz, Laurie Lynn Drummond, Marty Lammon, Bret Lott, Lee Martin, Joe Mackall, Robin Hemley, Brenda Miller, Mike Steinberg, Sue William Silverman, Rebecca Mc-Clanahan, Heather Sellers, Ladette Randolph, Natalia Rachel Singer, Diana Hume George, Richard Gilbert, Patrick Madden, Rebecca Skloot, Michael Rosenwald, Kristen Iversen, Steven Church, Lia Purpura, Scott Russell Sanders, Floyd Skloot, Rebecca Skloot, Bill Roorbach, Phil Gerard, Catherine Taylor, Kim Dana Kupperman, Sonya Huber, Marcia Aldrich, Robert Root, Patricia Foster, Michelle Herman, Nicole Walker, Margot Singer, and so many more, especially all of those who have contributed work and energy to *Brevity*.

Then there are the students, who teach me more than I teach them, particularly Rachael Peckham, Kelley Evans, Dave Wanczyk, Joey Franklin, Stephen David Grover, Liz Stephens, Jackson Connor, Kelly Ferguson, Ali Stine, Holly Baker, Amanda Dambrink, Kate Nuernberger, Jaswinder Bolina, Jolynn Baldwin, Kathleen Willis Morton, and Sonja Livingston,

Much gratitude as well to all of my teaching colleagues at Ohio University, but especially Mark Halliday, Jill Rosser, Joan Connor, Darrell Spencer, Zakes Mda, Kevin Haworth, and Joe McLaughlin.

To my wife Renita and daughter Maria, who put up with my disappearances into the writing office day after day after day.

And to my abused keyboard and beleaguered eyesight.

Sincere thanks, as well, to Scott Francis and Kelly Nickell at Writer's Digest Books, for their expert care and handling of this project.

And finally, thank you, thank you, thank you to all of the readers, of my work and of everyone else's work, because without readers, we writers would be a very sad lot of lonely people.